SHOSTAKOVICH: his life and times

SHOSTAKOVICH

his life and times

Eric Roseberry

MIDAS BOOKS

HIPPOCRENE BOOKS
New York

frontispiece
Shostakovich in his fifties listening to a rehearsal of one of his works
(Photograph loaned by Gennadi Rozhdestvensky)

In the same illustrated Series

BACH	Tim Dowley
BEETHOVEN	Ateş Orga
CHOPIN	Ateş Orga
DVORAK	Neil Butterworth
ELGAR	Simon Mundy
HAYDN	Neil Butterworth
MOZART	Peggy Woodford
OFFENBACH	Peter Gammond
PUCCINI	Peter Southwell-Sander
RACHMANINOFF	Robert Walker
SHOSTAKOVICH	Eric Roseberry
SCHUBERT	Peggy Woodford
SCHUMANN	Tim Dowley
TCHAIKOVSKY	Wilson Strutte
VERDI	Peter Southwell-Sander
General Editor:	William Eden

To Jill

First published UK in 1982 by
MIDAS BOOKS
12 Dene Way, Speldhurst, Tunbridge Wells, Kent TN3 0NX

ISBN 0 85936 144 6 (UK)

First published USA in 1982 by
HIPPOCRENE BOOKS
171 Madison Avenue, New York, NY10016

ISBN 0 88254 660 0 (US)

Printed and Bound in Great Britain
at The Pitman Press, Bath

Contents

1 Music as Documentary 7

2 The Year 1905 and its aftermath 16

3 A Petersburg Childhood (1906–1917) 28

4 The Year 1917 42

5 Schoolboy, Piano Student and Rising Young Composer (1917–1923) 54

6 The First Symphony — International Acclaim for a Soviet Genius (1924–1927) 64

7 The 'Modernist' Years: Stalin, Zhdanov and the First Reprimand (1927–1936) 75

8 Public and Private Artist (1934–1938) 88

9 Russia's Great Patriotic War. The Siege of Leningrad and the War Symphonies (1939–1945) 96

10 Zhdanov again and the Second Reprimand (1946–1953) 114

11 Death of Stalin and an artist's liberation — the Tenth Symphony (1953) 131

12 Composer Laureate — a Lenin Symphony at last. Cultural thaw and a new period of creative development (1954–1966) 143

13 Last works and death (1966–1975) 164

A Select Bibliography of Books available in English 182

A Select Discography 184

A Note on Sources 186

Acknowledgements and References 188

Index 190

Chapter 1

Music as Documentary

It is not the consciousness of men that determines their being, but, on the contrary, their social being that determines their consciousness. — Karl Marx

This twentieth century of ours has proved crueller than the preceding ones, nor did all its terrors end with its first fifty years. — Alexander Solzhenitsyn

If we have ears to hear, the life and times of Dmitri Dmitrievich Shostakovich are faithfully portrayed in his music. True, notes are not words, but for Shostakovich music was a report on human experience: his work records an eventful life and times with a sense of reality and sharpness of focus that belongs to the age of the photograph and the cinema. But this composer was no journalist in music — his musical training was in the old tradition of durable craftsmanship and his consciousness was deeply imbued with a sense of permanent values which he strove to express in music. In the words of a contemporary, 'The philosophical impact of Shostakovich's music is great, and who can tell but that it may one day acquaint our descendants with the spirit of our times more convincingly than dozens of ponderous volumes'. As we come to know the composer's personality through his music — in all its nervous tension, humour and tragic power — we sense a tough, heroic yet subtly personal and sensitive response to difficult and dangerous times, and a compassion for humanity that is overflowing but never sentimental.

If ever a country suffered in the twentieth century it was Russia, and in belonging to 'that great and tragic people' (as H. G. Wells called them) Shostakovich spent his formative years in the shadow of war and profound social upheaval. It is hardly surprising that one of his very first efforts at composition was a long piece called *Soldier*. 'Here the soldier shoots', wrote the ten year old Dmitri in his score, which contained 'a mass of illustrative detail and verbal explanations'. In 1917, the year of the revolution, he composed a *Funeral March on the victims of the Revolution*, inspired by a great

Kirov Theatre, Leningrad (Photograph loaned by Mrs. Olga Mair)

rally for the fallen in Petrograd attended by the young musician and his family. The same year Shostakovich suffered a traumatic experience which later found expression in his music. This was the killing of a boy by a Cossack during the street riots — apparently for nothing more than the theft of an apple. That incident was described in a passage in the second symphony: the listener is spared nothing of the swift brutality of the scene. 'I didn't forget that boy. And I never will', Shostakovich told his young friend, Solomon Volkov, in later life. From his parents and through his own reading, Shostakovich learnt of the shooting down of peaceful demonstrators by the Tsar's guards in Palace Square in January 1905, that event which by common consent marked the beginning of Russia's path to revolution and the overthrow of Imperial autocracy. In his eleventh symphony (1957) Shostakovich records the impact of that shocking event as if he had been an eye witness. And in the first movement of that same symphony, through the medium of ghostly political prisoners' songs, Shostakovich enshrines the whole spirit of oppressed, industrial Russia, crying out from the grave in its disquiet. (Like Dickens, or Dostoyevsky, Shostakovich had this inborn capacity to suffer with downtrodden humanity.) Military fanfares and tattoos, funeral march rhythms, dark, brooding melody, high-spirited frenzy, fierce, spitting outbursts of rage — these are some of the sound images of Shostakovich's war documentary style.

Quite early in his career as a musician Dmitri found an outlet for this inborn facility of musical response to life. As a student he had earned extra money for his hard-pressed family by playing the piano for silent films. The experience was unpleasant, but not without its bearing on his later composing style — a style that was at once realistic (in the sense of imitating sounds from real life) and full of hints, allusions, references to a wide range of music from all walks of life with which his audience might be expected to be familiar.

No less a feature of this simple yet complex music is its irony and wry humour — the contradiction between light-hearted expression and the fateful, tragic implications of the dramatic situation portrayed. In both his operas *Lady Macbeth* and *The Nose* such tensions are characteristic. As in the operas, so in the symphonies and instrumental music. Much of the gaiety is a mask, behind which may lurk painful emotion. Such is the 'light' music of the 'little' ninth symphony, which displeased Stalin who had wanted something in the grand tradition of ninth symphonies — heroic, monumental — to mark the end of the war. Such is the jaunty xylophone solo portraying the young soldier who is to die (seen through the pitying eyes of a self-sacrificing sister), in the fourteenth symphony. Shostakovich, living under the pressures of a totalitarian state which sought to discipline its artists to express a 'correct' Party view of life, had to learn to disguise his private feelings and be careful that romantic 'subjectivity' was not given too free a rein in a 'collectively-minded' society. Outwardly optimistic in their lively rhythms, the pitch tensions of the notes of his themes would sometimes tell a different story. (A simple test — try to whistle the 'jovial' opening theme of the fifteenth symphony.)

This is not to say that Shostakovich is always looking on the dark side of life (though sunshine is no more frequent in his music than it is in Leningrad). On the contrary, his sense of knock-about humour, the hopping gopak rhythms with which his dance finales can so often skip along, and the manic, sometimes grimful glee of sheer repetition for repetition's sake, can give his music a kind of Chaplin à la Russe quality, a readiness to play the fool in spite of everything. (Chaplin's own real-life style of humour and pathos—which was ever likely to spill into the Gogol-like fantasy—appealed strongly to the composer and his generation.)

Shostakovich, unlike his great contemporary colleagues in literature, Solzhenitsyn or Pasternak, was no dissident: he lived always at the centre of the political life of his country, devoting himself as a composer to the ideals of the Russian Revolution and the new State to which it gave birth. He willingly took up onerous official duties, becoming a Member of the Communist Party in

1960. Time and time again he had to listen to criticisms of his music, just or unjust, petty or well meant, but he never drew back from being true to himself, his audience and his players. He believed that music should bear a message, especially to his fellow countrymen, both as individuals and as members of a society that was born out of revolution. Although there were times, much to the disgust of more radical opponents of the régime, when he seemed to grovel in front of the cultural watch-dogs, his music remained, could not help remaining, his own.

Before Stalin came to power, the progressive young composer wrote music which sounded as bold as anything being heard in the West at the time. The twenties in Russia were an exciting period of ferment and experimentation in the Arts, and the Leningrad of 1927–28 was greatly influenced by the new music from abroad. Both Lenin and his enlightened Commissar of Culture and Education, Anatole Lunacharsky, had encouraged artistic freedom provided it aimed at serving the goals of a new society. It had already become fashionable to reject traditional techniques and outlooks. The poet Mayakovsky spoke of 'spitting out the past' which was 'like a bone stuck in our throats'; Malevich (who as early as 1914 had done his 'Composition with Mona Lisa') painted his 'Black Square' which has been interpreted as a blotting out of everything that had been before; Rodchenko took *his* point of

Malyi Opera Theatre, Leningrad (Photograph loaned by Mrs. Olga Mair)

departure from circles and lines — 'constructions'; there was also photography, the newly discovered technique of photo-montage, and the motion picture or 'movie' with Eisenstein as its exponent of genius; last, but by no means least, there was Meyerhold's theatre which became a veritable arsenal of avant garde techniques. Shostakovich was much influenced by these currents of thought and artistic activity in the late twenties, and he too shared the iconoclasm of his colleagues. His former teachers at the Conservatoire understood nothing of what he wrote in those days.

Then came the rise to power of Stalin who quickly put to an end this 'art without content', replacing it with the doctrine of 'Socialist Realism' which required, amongst other things, that Soviet art should reflect reality and concentrate on purpose with a capital 'P'. The Soviet Symphony now became a historical mission in which composers would give new life to a monumental form that, in the opinion of the ideologists, had become increasingly impossible to cultivate in Western capitalist society. Beethoven became a symbolic figure. For Shostakovich, who had explored for himself the symphonies of Mahler and Bruckner with his close friend Sollertinsky, the challenge was one he could meet. In his fifth symphony, written after the first big setback of his career (precipitated by Stalin's visit to a performance of *Lady Macbeth* in January 1936) the composer proved himself capable of handling themes in conflict on the large scale in a new, accessible, post-Mahlerian style. At one stroke, in music of a grand, epic simplicity, he established himself as a worthy successor to Beethoven, Mahler and Tchaikovsky. It set him on a road which, more than any other, was to secure him a great international reputation. In his 'heroic' symphonies Shostakovich, striving to express the new consciousness, actually applied the social/historical principles of Hegel and Marx: beginning with the fourth (which he withheld for over twenty-five years) these works embody philosophical ideas such as the identity of opposites and the dialectic of thesis, antithesis and synthesis. At the same time, his music was never cold and abstract, but strove to express life in all its contradictory aspects. Man remained at the centre of his work.

The second world war (or the Great Patriotic War, as it is known in Russia) saw Shostakovich as musical spokesman for a country once more called upon to endure cruel losses and destruction, though it has been said that this was nothing compared with Stalin's purges. Shostakovich's so-called 'War' symphonies, Nos. 7 and 8 in particular, are a direct expression of the spirit of a people at war, but perhaps also a continuing meditation on the theme of evil powers which all who suffered under the Stalin régime knew in a guise other than that of Hitler.

(Indeed, if Solomon Volkov is to be believed, the seventh symphony was conceived as a response to Stalin's terror long before the Nazi Siege of Leningrad.) Dedicated to the city of Leningrad, the seventh symphony came to symbolise the heroic spirit of that city which was under siege for 872 days, from September 8th 1941 to January 27th 1944. Nearly a million people perished from famine and enemy bombardment during those days. The eighth symphony, written during that same period, is another piece on the heroic scale, full of the grim imagery of mechanised war. Its last movement is very different from that of No. 7, winning through to a calm that is overcast with a sense of loss and desolation. For this reason it became controversial in official circles.

As soon as the war was over, Stalin's repression re-asserted itself and, at a notorious party conference presided over by Zdhanov in 1948, Shostakovich, in the company of Prokofiev and others, came in for further censure. Both the eighth and ninth symphonies had not pleased, and Shostakovich wisely withheld his next symphony (at this time he composed seriously for his desk drawer only) and dutifully turned his hand to the writing of film music.

With the death of Stalin it was possible to breathe freely again. On 17th December 1953 Shostakovich presented his long awaited tenth symphony, his most personal public work to date, in which the progression is from darkness to light, from a sense of brooding melancholy to individual high spirits. At last a genuinely happy ending seemed possible! In this symphony the initials of Shostakovich's name DSCH go up in lights, so to speak. (The letters DSCH from the German transliteration of the composer's name D(mitri) Sch(ostakovich) form the musical notes D, E flat, C and B.) Fittingly, the symphony was first performed in Leningrad, the composer's home city, at the end of its 250th anniversary celebrations. The work spoke for its time, just as did the Leningrad Symphony in 1942.

After Stalin, the country moved gradually into a period of cultural thaw — renewed contact with the West, exchange visits, a cautious welcoming of some of the newer trends in Western music —though in the capricious peasant-like utterances of Khrushchev cultural ideologists could never be quite sure of their ground. A new term gained currency — 'rehabilitation'; and two of Shostakovich's banned works *Lady Macbeth* (now renamed *Katerina Ismailova*) and the fourth symphony (which, it will be remembered, the composer himself had withdrawn in 1936) were now heard. Their impact at home and abroad was stunning, heightened, if anything, by their period of banishment. Both of them showed that they had withstood the test of time.

As the thaw progressed, and after two October Revolution Commemorative works, the eleventh and twelfth symphonies (1957 and 1961 respectively) Shostakovich, in collaboration with a young poet, Yevgeni Yevtushenko, spoke out courageously, using words for the first time in a symphony since 1929. In his eighth quartet, written after a visit to the war-ravaged city of Dresden, he had denounced the evils of Fascism; now he spoke out against these same evils in Russian society itself, attacking anti-Semitism as unpatriotic, praising non-conformity as personified in the movement called 'Humour', and applauding the stance of Galileo, Shakespeare, Pasteur and Tolstoy who stuck to the truth instead of looking to their career prospects. The intensely Russian style of Shostakovich's address in this symphony gave it a special popular appeal: at its première it was wildly cheered, but fell into immediate official disfavour. Shostakovich, taking advantage of the liberal climate, in his capacity of *yurodivy* (the traditional 'holy fool' who is allowed to speak unpalatable truths to his ruler) had overstepped the mark. (The Fool in *King Lear* was one of Shostakovich's favourite characters, and he had set his verses with great relish for a Leningrad production of the play in 1941).

From now on Shostakovich turned to more private themes. He had in any case written much music apart from the symphonies, of an intimate, confessional nature. The String Quartet (Shostakovich had by this time written eight) became even more of a diary into which the composer confided secret, private thoughts.

Leningrad Conservatoire — Opera Studio (Photograph loaned by Mrs. Olga Mair)

(Nos. 7 and 9 were, significantly, dedicated to members of his family, the former to the memory of his first wife Nina Vasilyevna who died early, the latter to his third wife, Irena Suprinskaya.) These quartets, and certain other highly personal and 'non-ideological' works such as the two cello concertos, reveal in all its strength this strange and complex personality — laconic yet expansive, introspective yet manically extrovert, compassionate yet cruel. The moods are equivocal, enigmatic. And yet these moods are controlled — as always in Shostakovich — by an unfailing structural sense of unity, classical balance and continuity. The ear of the composer matches, as it were, the architectural spirit of Peter the Great's symphony in stone which was St Petersburg.

As the composer moved into a sick and frail old age, fêted, universally acclaimed, yet not altogether approved of by the Soviet cultural bureaucracy despite its collective pride in their one indisputably international composer of genius (Prokoviev, Shostakovich's only rival had, ironically enough, died on the same day as Stalin) he turned to darker utterances, to a pre-occupation with images of death. The terror and personal isolation of the late quartets, especially Nos. 13 and 15, the bleak celebration of death as an all-powerful figure in the fourteenth symphony, the journey into eternity of the Viola Sonata (his last completed composition)

Glinka Concert Hall, Leningrad (Photograph loaned by Mrs. Olga Mair)

and, not least, the Prospero-like farewell of his last completed symphony (in which so much of his past achievement is reviewed in retrospect) with its sharp awareness of the imminence of death's stroke — all this music is the self expression of one who, like Mahler before him in his dark trilogy of late works, needed to come to terms with the physical reality of life's end. There are no heroics in these energetic and technically assured works, nor is there self pity, rather a capacity to reflect and record unflinchingly the inevitability of our common fate. There is even humour, for Shostakovich could joke, too, with the grim reaper as he had already demonstrated in his second cello concerto — a work that offers no illusory comforts in a sad world. In all these late works, in addition to the ubiquitous funeral march motif, there is the recurrent mediaeval image beloved of Liszt and the nineteenth century romantics, of the danse macabre, the *Totentanz* which had fascinated Shostakovich as a young man in his early, iconoclastic *Aphorisms* for piano.

There was one consolation as death approached — that of his work, which would survive him and speak for him and his times. Increasingly, Shostakovich's art acquired a sense of monumental epitaph. In the last song of the *Verses of Michelangelo* Shostakovich speaks through the Renaissance poet, accompanied by a child-like symbol of immortality, a little dance played on the piccolo:

I shall live on in the hearts and minds of people.

And this Shostakovich does. Like Goya, Dickens, Tolstoy and Pasternak he was both of his time and for all times. More than any other twentieth century composer since Mahler, his work, especially that of his middle period symphonies, Nos. 5-13, bears comparison with Beethoven in its revolutionary idealism and broad humanity. And, like Beethoven, he composed a testament of last quartets. It was Soviet society and politics that helped to create the phenomenon of Shostakovich, that defined him as an artist who had to grapple with the problems of Soviet controls; but his unique creative personality, his human individuality, was the gift of his parents, to whom, as he once said in an official speech, he owed 'everything good'.

His parents were in their early thirties, living in No. 2, Podolskaya Street, St Petersburg, with their first child, Marusia, when the Tsarist Russia of their generation suffered its first severe tremors. The year 1905 is the prologue to the composer's life story.

Chapter 2

The Year 1905 and its aftermath

Our family discussed the revolution of 1905 constantly . . . the stories deeply affected my imagination. When I was older, I read much about how it all happened.

Shostakovich to Volkov in *Testimony*

Nicholas II, who had become Emperor of Russia in October 1894, found himself caught up in social and political forces beyond his control: he inherited the revolution. That inheritance was summed up by Leon Trotsky with admirable concision. In one brief paragraph he encapsulated the five decades in which Russia moved — with lightning rapidity — towards emancipation:

The political development of Russia, beginning with the middle of the last century, is measured by decades. The sixties — after the Crimean War — were an epoch of enlightenment, our short lived eighteenth century. During the following decade the intelligentsia were already endeavouring to draw practical conclusions from the theories of enlightenment. The decade began with the movement going down to the people with revolutionary propaganda; it ended with terrorism. The seventies passed into history mainly as the years of 'The People's Will'. The best elements of that generation went up in the blaze of the dynamite warfare. The enemy had held all its positions. Then followed a decade of decline, of disenchantment and pessimism, of religious and moral searchings — the eighties. Under the veil of reaction, however, the forces of capitalism were blindly at work. The nineties brought with them workers' strikes and Marxist ideals. The new tide reached its culmination in the first decade of the new century — in the year 1905.

1905, the year before the composer was born, began ominously with a massacre which put an end to any hopes for a peaceful solution to Imperial Russia's problems.

January 9th (OS)* — 'Bloody Sunday', as it came to be called —

Father Gapon leading petitioners to the Tsar in 1905 (Novosti)

*Soviet Russia adopted the New Style (Gregorian) Calendar at the end of January, 1918, thus ending a 13 day discrepancy between Russia and the West which had always obtained under the Tsars. January 9th 1905, was therefore January 22nd outside Russia.

was the first and most dramatic of a series of confrontations between people and Imperial autocracy which gathered force in that year, ending with a no less bloodily suppressed uprising in Moscow. On that day a priest, Father Gapon (who had the ear of both the people and the authorities) led a procession of workers and their families through the streets of St Petersburg to present a petition to the Tsar at the Winter Palace. This petition, respectfully but firmly worded, sought improved working conditions and governmental reform. Nicholas II was not, however, in residence that day. Instead, he had left orders with his police and militia to deal firmly with any threat to law and order — and things got out of hand all over St Petersburg.

The central, catastrophic incident was in Palace Square. Boris Pasternak, with a poet's feeling for atmosphere, describes it, and certain preceding events, in a sequence of vivid, disjointed images which impress themselves on the mind's eye like photo montage in an Eisenstein film.

A Petersburg night.
A moon
like a crisp
new crown
and a glassy clink
as the strange crowd
tramples the air,
when dudes and scavengers
meet
in the Tsar's own town
to hear
Father Gapon
lay the national
misery
bare.

There's a roar
in the hall
a forest
of swaying heads,
five thousand fighting for breath.
The wind
in its rage
whines
at the door of this crèche:
five thousand beds
puckered and raw
but
undisguised
lusty
new age.

A notorious trollop
of dawn
bruised berries —
the clouds:
a vapour of sewerage
muffling the murmuring feet
as they crowd
with their makeshift
banners
(or fancies
or shrouds)
from the hall
to the blistering fires
of the frostbrittle street.

A marvellous river of people.
Muttering thunder.
Hats off, men and pray —
for your leader
the priest
is astute.
To the left is the palace
to the right is God's acre
but under your noses
awaiting you,
His Majesty's Royal Salute!

Windows are in leaf
lamp-standards
budded with faces
admiring those endless

cohorts of the marchers
break through the blocks at
the crossroads
sweep easy
by open spaces
swell
by the bridge at the Palace
to a beautiful lake.

Then —
nine
harsh
volleys
shatter
that mirror of waters
the last sound
dawdling
in echoes as
bedraggled as
glory,
and the sea of heads froths to a panic
and the wail of the slaughter
fills the far skies
with its eddies
persistent
and gory.

The sidewalks
in flight,
the brief day
shattered for ever . . .
To imperial gunners
from barricades
the response.

In Shostakovich's eleventh symphony (composed just over half a century after the massacre) there is a no less vivid evocation in sound of the symbolic drama. The snowbound emptiness of the Palace Square is the stage set for the tragedy: the interweaving of military fanfares and workers' songs creates an atmosphere of brooding tension. And now Pasternak's 'marvellous river of people muttering thunder' arrives in a determined mood, singing as they march a prayer to their Tsar in whom they are still prepared to believed.

Oh, Tsar, our little father,
Look around you;
Life is impossible for us because of the Tsar's servants,
Against whom we are helpless . . .

Crowds in a St Petersburg Street, 1905 (Novosti)

Palace Square, 1905. The Tsar's troops fire on the workers (Novosti)

The prayer to the Tsar becomes more insistent and turbulent — there have already been shootings on the way to the Palace and the people are not easily going to be turned away. They confront the Imperial Palace Guard in a tense moment of stillness in Palace Square. The shooting breaks out and the crowd begins to run as the victims fall. We hear the despairing cries and groans, the tumultuous panic as the military assert their pitiless supremacy amidst the smoke and din. Suddenly it is silent again, but the silence is now one of numb horror as we contemplate the scene. A terrible, irrevocable crime against the Russian people has been committed.

Shostakovich's symphonic documentary of 1905 continues with the Revolutionary Funeral Hymn *You fell as victims* which Lenin and his comrades sang in exile in Zürich on hearing the news of Bloody Sunday. Here is Lenin's widow's account of how the news was received:

The Battleship Potemkin, 1905. An oil painting of a scene from the mutiny by K. G. Dorokhov (Novosti)

The news of the January 9th events reached Geneva the morning after. Vladimir Ilyich and I were on our way to the library and met the Lunacharskys, who were on their way to us. I remember the figure of Lunacharsky's wife, Anne Alexandrovna, who was so excited that she could not speak, but only helplessly wave her muff. We went where all the Bolsheviks who had heard the Petersburg news were instinctively drawn — to the Lepeshinskys' emigrant restaurant. We wanted to be

The Battleship Potemkin, 1905. 'Its stark, geometrical beauty distinguishing it, a powerful battleship lies in the anchorage . . .' A still from Eisenstein's 'Constructivist' film of 1925 (Novosti)

together. The people gathered there hardly spoke a word to one another, they were so excited. With tense faces they sang the Revolutionary Funeral March. Everyone was overwhelmed with the thought that the Revolution had already started, that the bonds of faith in the Tsar were broken, that now the time was quite near when 'tyranny will fall, and the people will rise up — great, mighty and free.'

Bloody Sunday was a spark which lit many fires. Russia was at war with Japan — a Tsar's war that had little genuine patriotic appeal — and the discontent of soldiers and sailors with the conduct of that disastrous war was fanning the flames of social unrest at home, especially in the cities where huge concentrations of workers were losing patience — and waking up to political consciousness through their Soviets, or Workers' Councils. A resounding naval defeat at Tsushima in May had left the ordinary sailors of the Russian fleet with little appetite for further fighting. Mutinies broke out, of which the most stirring in its appeal to popular imagination was that on board the battleship *Potemkin*, where a whole crew turned against its officers and sailed the sea unharmed despite Imperial orders for its interception by other ships. Peace with Japan was negotiated in September at the Treaty of Portsmouth. By October the country was completely paralysed by strikes: never before had there existed such a potent solidarity between workers, revolutionaries and young intellectuals. There was plenty of sympathy for their cause amongst the liberal intellegentsia, to which class belonged the Shostakovich family who had, in the composer's words, *Narodnik* (or 'populist') leanings.

Student demonstration on the University Embankment in St Petersburg, 1905 (Novosti)

The Tsar, in urgent consultation with his able minister Count de Witte, newly ennobled after negotiating the peace treaty, was obliged to consider the plight of his tottering administration. Writing to his mother, he related the choice de Witte placed before him:
either

> to appoint an energetic military man and try with all the force at our disposal to put the sedition down. This would give us a breathing space, and then in a few months' time we should have to use force again. But this would mean shedding rivers of blood and it would lead in the end back to the present position. . . .

Alternatively

> to grant civil rights to the population — the freedom of speech, of the press, of assembly, and association and the inviolability of the person, and, apart from that, an undertaking to submit every legislative proposal to the State Duma, which means in effect a constitution. Witte argued vigorously in favour of this course, saying that, although it involved some risk, it was the only possible one at the present moment.

The Tsar was forced to take 'the frightful decision' and, on 17th October (OS) he signed the document known as 'The October Manifesto' which, in principle, conceded the handing over of power to the Russian people. The document stated that Nicholas had ordered the Government

Firstly: to grant the people the fundamental civil liberties;
Secondly: to admit immediately to participation in the State Duma . . . those classes of the population which are now completely deprived of electoral rights,
Thirdly: to establish as an inviolable rule that no law may become effective without the consent of the State Duma.
We call on all faithful sons of Russia . . . to remember their duty to their Fatherland, to assist in putting an end to these unprecedented disturbances, and to make with Us every effort to restore peace and quiet to Our native land.

Thus, as Trotsky wrote, 'the revolution won its first victory, a victory not complete in itself, but one which promised much'. Trotsky had arrived in St Petersburg when the October strike was at its peak, to take part in the St Petersburg Soviet of Workers which had held its first meeting four days before the issue of the Imperial Manifesto. He wrote:

the day after the promulgation of the manifesto, tens of thousands of people were standing in front of the University of St Petersburg, aroused by the struggle and intoxicated with the joy of their first victory. I shouted to them from the balcony not to trust an incomplete victory, that the enemy was stubborn, that there were traps ahead; I tore the Tsar's manifesto into pieces and scattered them to the winds. But such political warnings only scratch the surface of the mass consciousness. The masses need the schooling of big events.

The social revolution was losing its momentum, and it was now only a matter of time before the Tsar was able to regain control, thanks largely to the Army and Police which were called in to deal with the final agonised spasm of revolt in 1905 — a workers' uprising in Moscow which was put down with characteristic brutality. Civilised opinion the world over was shocked by the mass executions and reprisals that took place there in December. Shostakovich's Aunt Nadejda (sister of his mother) was actually in Moscow caring for the wounded at that time, and later, in 1917, she was able to tell her eleven year old nephew of the heroism of the Moscow revolutionists.

They erected clumsy barricades and defended themselves with revolvers against the machine guns that had been hoisted on the belfries of the cathedrals . . .

On the barricades, Moscow 1905. A painting by I. Vladimirov (SCR)

Prisoners were executed without trial; houses and factories were bombarded and destroyed; the terrorised population was treated like a conquered enemy. Not satisfied with its military triumphs, the government sent its soldiers on a punitive expedition into the Moscow region. The orders from the high authorities: 'Take no prisoners; act without mercy,' were carried out to the letter.

The same month — on 3rd December (OS) the St Petersburg Soviet and its leaders were arrested and imprisoned. Trotsky and his associates were sent first to the Kresty Prison, then the Peter-Paul Fortress and finally to the House of Preliminary Detention. Their trial in St Petersburg was to take place in September 1906, the month of Dmitri's birth. The sentence: removal of all civic rights and enforced settlement in exile. (Trotsky was, in fact, to escape on his way to Siberia).

It was a strange, contradictory time. Despite the rigid enforcement of law and order in the cruel hands of the Tsar's new

Rimsky Korsakov — one of the last portraits. (Shostakovich's teacher, M. O. Steinberg, was a close disciple of the master and married his daughter) (Novosti)

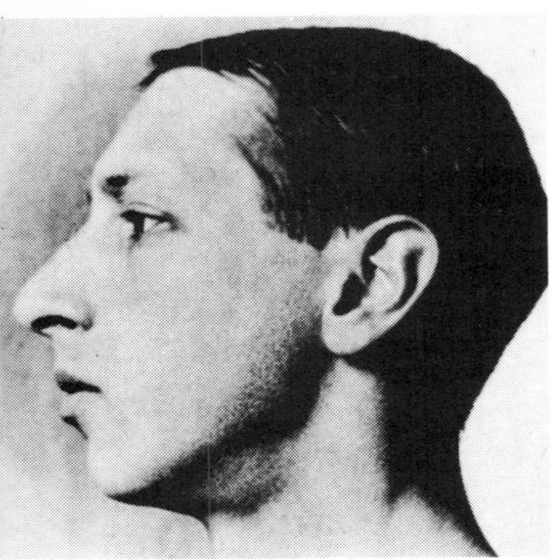

The young Stravinsky, pupil of Rimsky Korsakov. His first symphony, Op.1, was produced in St Petersburg in 1908 (Novosti)

minister, Stolypin, and the deep resentment of the families of the bereaved and oppressed, there was, through the first Duma, a 'stimulation of political life'. 'Revolution and counter revolution were still in the balance' wrote Trotsky, and much had been learnt from the Russian people's first attempt to take power. While Nicholas appeared to have learnt nothing (he was to dissolve the first Duma after 73 days of its political life) this 'dress rehearsal' for the decisive later revolution of 1917 had taught his opponents a good deal. Above all, they realised that nothing could be achieved without the support of the Army (on which the Tsar could still rely) and, in this respect, history was to play into their hands with the war of 1914. The mobilisation of support amongst Russia's huge peasant population was, however, to remain a problem: Stolypin cunningly set about serving the Tsar's best interests through selling them State owned land — a policy which the revolutionaries saw as a serious threat to their cause, which had to depend to a large extent on the factory workers in towns. But Stolypin was to be killed by an assassin's bullet in 1911 — and the revolutionary movement (both in and out of Russia) revived in the climate of an increasingly lax and corrupt administration.

For Shostakovich's parents life went on as before, and music was a very important part of their family life, as it was in the capital itself. Rimsky Korsakov, after becoming something of a student revolutionary cult figure through a performance of his opera *Kaschei the Immortal* in March 1905, had been dismissed from his post as Head of the Conservatoire and in December Glazunov had replaced him, accepting the position on condition that Rimsky Korsakov was re-instated at the Conservatoire. A brilliant pupil of Rimsky Korsakov, Igor Stravinsky by name, was shortly to produce his first symphony that was to be dedicated to his master. Another young fire-brand, Sergei Prokofiev, was studying at the Conservatoire, impatient with his harmony lessons. In the cultural traffic that went on freely between St Petersburg and the West (especially Paris) a young entrepreneur of genius, Sergei Diaghilev, was inspired to organise a festival of Russian music in Paris. (He was already notorious for his views on 'art for art's sake' as proclaimed in a journal *Mir Iskustva* [The World of Art] that he and Alexander Benois had founded). In St Petersburg itself could be heard the music of the European avant garde — Reger, Mahler, Richard Strauss, Schoenberg, Debussy, Ravel. Noteable first performances abroad of the year 1905 had included Mahler's *Kindertotenlieder* in Vienna, Debussy's *La Mer* in Paris and Strauss's *Salome* in Dresden. Of Debussy's *Pelléas et Mélisande* (1902) which Rimsky Korsakov was to hear in 1907 in Paris we learn that the grand old man of Russian music would have 'nothing more to do with this music lest I should unhappily

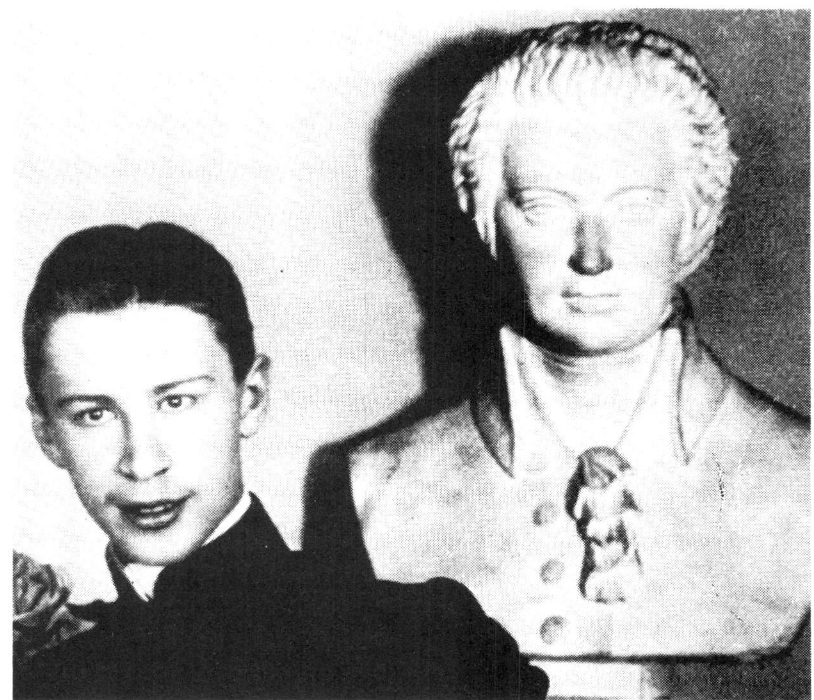

Prokofiev at the St Petersburg Conservatory in 1908. 'His lusty young young voice first sounded at the beginning of the century, and throughout the following years it could be distinctly heard above the din and clangour of that eventful period in music.' (Shostakovich in 1954) (Novosti)

develop a liking for it'. And, curiously enough, of all European composers, Debussy was the one composer whose music remained completely alien to Shostakovich. Of the French Impressionists' influence there was to be not a trace — for reasons which will later become apparent. For not dissimilar reasons the music of Russia's own Scriabin — a highly popular figure — was to be discounted by the post-revolutionaries. But we are telling of a time when music and politics were allowed to go their own separate ways: Dmitri Shostakovich was to reach maturity as a composer in a different climate.

Chapter 3

A Petersburg Childhood (1906–1917)

I love you, city of Peter's creation,
I love your stern, harmonious aspect,
The majestic flow of the Neva,
Her granite banks,
The iron tracery of your railings,
The transparent twilight
And the moonless gleam of your pensive nights.

Pushkin – The Bronze Horseman

'Cities are the only source of inspiration for a truly modern, contemporary art' wrote Pasternak in *Dr Zhivago*, '. . . the living language of our time is urban.' Dmitri Dmitrievich* Shostakovich was born and bred a townsman in what was then the chief town of Russia — St Petersburg. He shared the sights, sounds and climate of this great city with other creative artists of his time. With Akhmatova, the poetess, who felt bound to this 'sombre town on the menacing current . . . quiet, beclouded, austere'; with Meyerhold, the theatre director who, all his life 'dreamed of producing a Greek tragedy in Leningrad in the square in front of the Kazan Cathedral'; with Rodchenko, the constructivist, whose revolutionary inspiration was urban through and through in his posters, collages and spatial constructions. We are concerned with a composer for whom, as he grew up, streets, shops, theatres, bridges, statues, crowds, great vistas, waterways, heroic sky lines, 'white' nights, a visual, architectural sense of continuity with the past in conflict with a social rejection of that same past, were daily experiences.

St Petersburg was the creation of Peter the Great who built his 'window on the West' at the cost of untold millions of lives at the turn of the seventeenth century. The granite stone of its foundations (the town had been built on a swamp) was imported in the form of a tax on everyone who came to live and work there. It is

The Bronze Horseman. Monument to Peter the Great, founder of the City of St Petersburg (SCR)

*In Russia, people are given a first name (eemya) and patronymic (otchestvo) derived from the father's name.

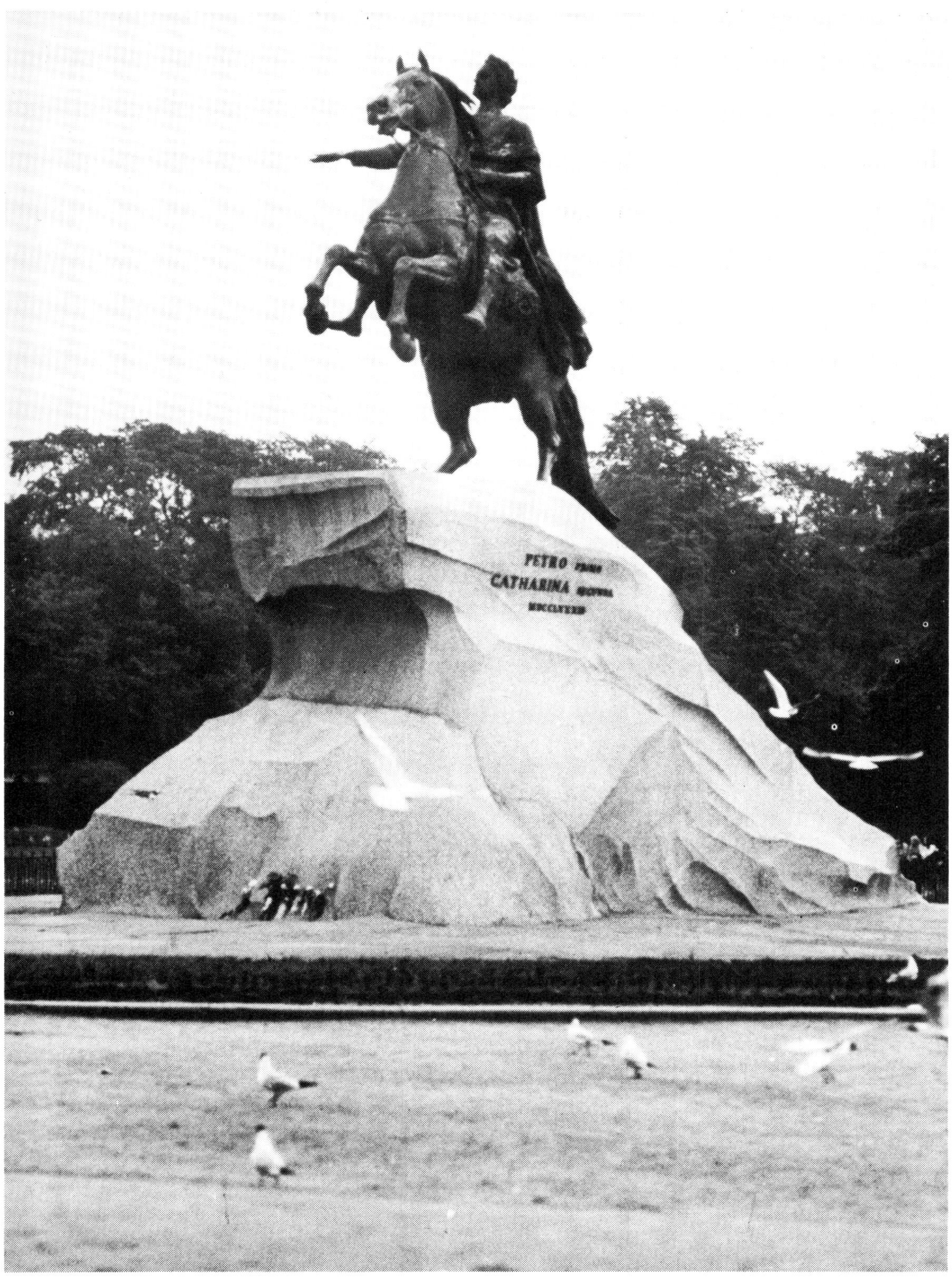
PETRO
CATHARINA

said that every stone represented the life of a worker, so that its architectural severity and grace were built on human suffering on the large scale. Pushkin sensed a duality about the atmosphere of this city. In his poem *The Bronze Horseman* — a tale of the time of a terrible flood in 1825 — the bog gods of the swamp struggle to take back from the bronze Tsar what had originally belonged to them. Pushkin, in Nabokov's words, 'had noticed the queer pale green tint of its skies and the mysterious energy of the bronze Tsar rearing his steed against a fluid background in a wilderness of wide streets and spacious squares.' Nineteenth century industrialisation came comparatively late to Russia and in that process a city which was originally conceived as a harmonious symphony in stone became transformed into something less desirable, more sinister and complex. 'The white mists of the Neva were blackened by the fog of factory chimneys' wrote Alexander Werth as he reflected on the city's past during the Nazi siege of 1941. 'Instead of the crisp, sunny winter days of Pushkin came the eerie rainy autumn nights of Dostoyevsky and the shadowy unreality of Blok's St Petersburg poem.' And before his death in 1909, Innokenti Annensky wrote his tragic prophecy — his poem *St Petersburg* — in which he spoke of Peter's 'cursed error . . . a city of cadaverous yellow water, yellow snow'.

But the same writer has given us a much more affectionate — even romantic — portrait of this Petersburg before the first world war — the Petersburg of Shostakovich's parents and early childhood.

I loved St Petersburg, and the Summer Garden with its centenarian lime trees, and the little house of Peter the Great, and the alley of Greek gods and goddesses with their chipped noses . . . and the majestic sweep of the Neva, with the lofty, graceful spire of the Fortress silhouetted against the 'white' summer night. I remember the smells and the sounds of St Petersburg; the clatter of trotting hooves on the wooden pavements of the Mokhovaia; it was the first sound you heard when you woke in the morning; the jam of horse traffic in the Simeonovskoya, with the carters . . . swearing obscenely at their horses and at their fellow carters; and I can still smell the hot tar of the road-mending squads in midsummer . . .

And Mahler, writing to his wife from Petersburg in 1907 during rehearsals of his 5th symphony, asks if she remembers 'the peculiar smell there is in Russia everywhere, even on the railway. A mixture of woodsmoke and Russian leather . . . '

Shostakovich has left us no personal description of the St Petersburg he grew up in, but we are fortunate in having some vivid reminiscences of late nineteenth century Petersburg, before the electric trams of Shostakovich's childhood, by Igor

Stravinsky, who loved the place of his childhood and youth as only an expatriate can:

St Petersburg street noises are especially vivid to me . . . The first such sounds to record themselves on my awareness were those of droshkies on cobblestone, or block-wood parquetry pavements. Only a few of these horse carriages had rubber tyres, and these few were doubly expensive; the whole city crackled with the iron-hooped wheels of the others. I also remember the sound of horse-drawn streetcars and, in particular, the rail-scraping noise they made as they turned the corner near our house and whipped up speed to cross the Krukov Canal Bridge. (Steeper bridges sometimes required the use of extra horses, and those were found at hitching posts throughout the city.) The noises of wheels and horses and the shouts and whipcracks of coachmen must have penetrated my earliest dreams; they are, at any rate, my first memory of the streets of childhood. (The clatter of automobiles and electric trolley cars, two decades later, was much less memorable . . .)

The loudest diurnal noises of the city were the cannonade of bells from the Nikolsky Cathedral, and the noon signal from the Peter and Paul Fortress — a timepiece for the whole populace . . .

A city is also remembered by its odours. In the case of St Petersburg, these were associated chiefly with droshkies. They smelled agreeably of tar, of leather, and of their horses. Usually, however, the strongest odour emanated from the driver himself . . .

One other aroma that permeated the city and, indeed, all Russia, was of the tobacco called Mahorka; it was originally imported by Peter the Great.

I remember St Petersburg as an ochre city (in spite of such prominent red buildings as the Winter Palace and Anichkov Palace), the architecture, as well as the colour, of St Petersburg, was Italian, and Italian not merely by imitation but by the direct work of such architects as Quarenghi and Rastrelli.

Italian stylization and craftsmanship could be found in any work of the Catherine the Great period, whether in a building, a statue, or an *objet d'art*. And the principal palaces were Italian not only in design but in material (marble). Even in the case of the ordinary St Petersburg building stone, which was a local granite or an equally local brick, the outer surfaces were plastered, and painted Italian colours.

The Marinsky Theatre was a delight to me. To enter the blue-and-gold interior of that heavily-perfumed hall was, for me, like entering the most sacred of temples.

St Petersburg was a city of islands and rivers. The latter were called Neva, mostly — Great Neva, Small Neva, Great Small Neva, Middle Neva. The movements of boats and the life of the harbour are less significant in my recollections than one might expect, however, because of the long, icebound winters.

St Petersburg was also a city of large, open piazzas. One of these, the Champs de Mars, might have been the scene of *Petroushka*.

Another attractive piazza was the Haymarket, where hundreds of wains were stored to supply the city's huge horse population; to walk there was to be reminded of the countryside. But my most animated promenades in St Petersburg were on the Nevsky Prospekt, a wide avenue, three miles long, and full of life and movement all the way. Here were the beautiful Stroganov Palace (by Rastrelli); the Lutheran Church (which Balakirev, a devout Orthodoxist, used to call the upside-down

trousers); the Kazansky Cathedral, with its semicircle of columns in imitation of St Peter's in Rome; the Duma (City Hall); the Gastinny Dvor (Merchants' Court), a block of arcades with hundreds of shops; the Public Library; the Drama Theatre; and the Anichkov Palace, Tsar Alexander III's residence. The Nevsky Prospekt was also the principal arena for amorous assignations, and at night it was full of 'grues', and the officers and students who were their chief customers. A letter of Leon Bakst's to me in Morges in 1915: '. . . you remember how in the Nevsky Prospect, on a beautiful, white, Russian night, the purple-painted whores yell after you, "men, give us cigarettes".'

Another feature of the city, whose inhabitants are ever conscious of the river and its moods, is the 'running of the ice' each Spring — an image which inspired Stravinsky's *Rite*. Here is the account of a closer contemporary, Nikolai Malko, of that event:

The first ice takes a customary course: the spring sun becomes warmer, the ice on the river gets darker, swells, cracks threateningly, splits, and then suddenly starts to move in one great relentless mass. The huge pieces of ice drift slowly forward, pushing against each other and smashing into the banks: the cracking sounds and the rattling can be heard for miles. Bridges and quais are full of people enjoying this magnificent and incomparable sight. In the course of three or four days the Neva is completely cleared of ice. A commander's cutter makes its customary run to the Winter Palace, and navigation is officially opened. Warm, beautiful, sunny days then come to Leningrad, but only for about three weeks. Suddenly, one morning, a foggy and depressing air bears down on the city, and everything is changed. Again it becomes chilly, and icy sleet starts falling. The Lake Ladoga ice is running the Neva. It moves slowly, lazily, not like the first run of a single mass, but in separate, broken pieces and conglomerate heaps. And so it is for about three days. The entire city starts coughing and sneezing. Influenza runs rampant. No trace of the recent joyous mood remains. Then, just as suddenly as it came, this spell ends. The air freshens and becomes pure; the sun is really warm. The beautiful Neva is once again free and clear. From time to time, still, a single dirty chunk of ice appears along the banks, but is just an unnoticed and forgotten remnant.

The parents-to-be of the composer had come to this St Petersburg as students in 1900. Sophia Vasilyevna Kokaoulin, the composer's mother, was the daughter of a manager of the Lena Gold Fields at Bodaybo in Siberia, responsible to the St Petersburg adminstration for the efficient running of the work force there. Vassily, her father, with his wife brought up their family of six children in this remote outpost, attending to their daily duties with a kindness and humanity that endeared them to the community of miners and their families. Patriarchal Vassily may have been (he was certainly no revolutionary sympathiser) but his progressive views (strikingly akin to those of the young Tolstoy) on improving the quality and conditions of life of these people earned him their approval and respect. A saying proudly quoted in the Shostakovich family after the 1912 massacre of workers in the Lena Gold Fields ran to the effect that such a catastrophe could never have occurred there during Vassily's time. Sophia was given the privileged education of a well-to-do girl of the managerial classes. She was sent in 1890 to the Irkutsk Institute for Noblewomen founded by Tsar Nicholas I where fear of God and loyalty to the royal family were inculcated as cardinal virtues. When Nicholas II visited the school as Crown Prince she was presented to him and danced the Mazurka from Glinka's *A Life for the Czar.* She was a good musician, reaching a standard of proficiency on the piano that qualified her for admission to the Petersburg Conservatoire shortly after the family returned to Russia in 1898 when her father resigned his post at Bodaybo. With her in St Petersburg were her sister Nadejda, at the Bestuzhev College for Women, and Jasha, a brilliant brother at the University, deeply involved in the student revolutionary movement.

Workers demonstrate after the massacre at Lena, 1912 (Novosti)

Dmitri Boleslavovich Shostakovich, father of the composer (Novosti)

It was at a musical party given at the Gamboyevs where she lodged as a student, that Sophia met her future husband, Dmitri Boleslavovich Shostakovich. Dmitri, 'about five feet five, rather stocky, with light brown hair, a light moustache and a pair of dark brown eyes' was a student of histology at the University, very fond of music and full of fun. He had a good voice, too, and was very ready to oblige, accompanied at the piano by Sophia, with arias from the Tchaikovsky operas and the popular drawing room romances of the day. Dmitri's family also came from Siberia — but from a very different background of political exile. The family name Shostakovich is Polish, and Russia's relationship

A map of St Petersburg in 1908, by which time electric trams had come to the City. Podolskaya Street is ref. 6-K. Nikolaevskaya Street, where the family moved in 1910, is ref. 3-H. (Reproduced by permission of the British Library. BL.Maps 47.a.28)

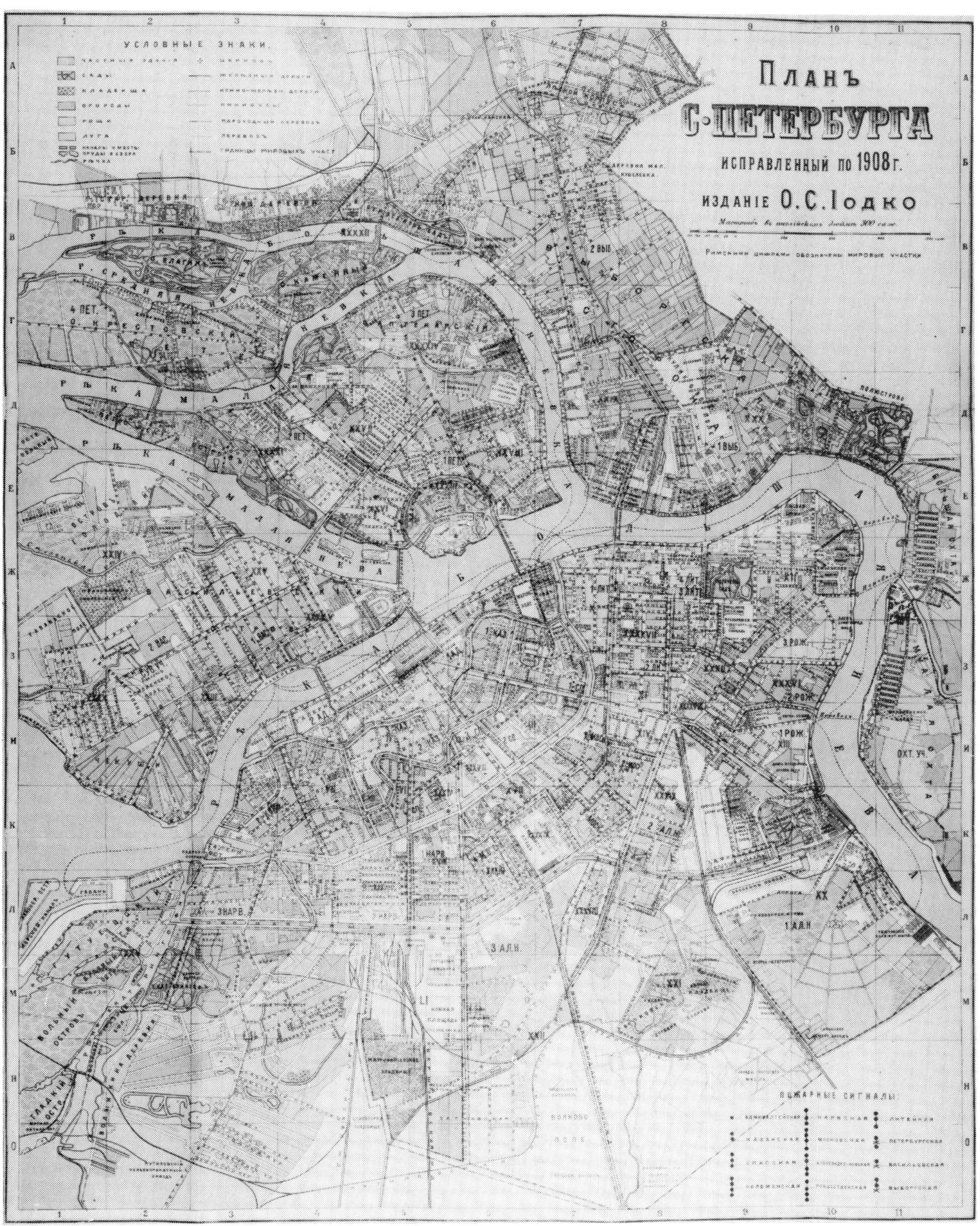

ПЛАНЪ
С.-ПЕТЕРБУРГА
ИСПРАВЛЕННЫЙ ПО 1908Г.
ИЗДАНIЕ О.С. IОДКО
Римскими цифрами обозначены мировые участки
УСЛОВНЫЕ ЗНАКИ.
ПОЖАРНЫЕ СИГНАЛЫ:

Podolskaya Street, birthplace of the composer. (Drawing by David Cook after a photograph)

with Poland as a colony of Russian Imperialism had been a stormy and repressive one. Dmitri's great grandfather had taken part in the Polish uprising of 1830 and was sent into exile after the taking of Warsaw; his father had been active in the insurrection of 1863–4 and had been arrested for hiding a revolutionary who was later hanged. Narim, where Dmitri had been brought up, was an exiles' camp and his father had been sent there, together with others implicated in the plot, after the assassination of Alexander II in 1881.

It can readily be seen that such a name and such a family background would not perhaps readily recommend itself to the parents of a daughter who had graduated with the Chiffre award — a mark of social distinction in Tsarist Russia. But times were changing, and, besides, the young man was both attractive and no violent revolutionary in outlook himself. The young couple were married on 31st January, 1903, and their first child — a daughter, Marusia — was born in October the same year. (A second daughter, Zoya, was born in 1908.) Sophia had relinquished her musical studies on marrying and her husband had taken up a post at the Petersburg Chamber of Weights and Measures where, as a chemical engineer, he was a colleague of the famous Russian scientist Dmitri Ivanovich Mendeleyev — a fact which the composer would recall with pride. They had found themselves an apartment at No. 2 Podolskaya Street, close to the husband's place of work, where their only son was to be born three years later.

Mitya with his sister Marusia in 1907 (Novosti)

The composer's mother, Sophia Vassilevna, with her three children in 1909 (Novosti)

Dmitri, the composer, was born at 5 p.m. on 12th September 1906. There are no reports of uncommon musical ability in the cradle, though the sounds of family music making were in his ears from the start. Childhood reminiscences from the composer himself are sparse — indeed, on one occasion he is reported as saying that 'my childhood had no significant or outstanding incidents'. But certain events did impress themselves on his memory. Amongst his first recollections were musical evenings in a neighbouring apartment where an enthusiastic amateur cellist, an engineer, would meet his friends for quartet playing. 'He often played quartets and trios by Mozart, Beethoven, Borodin and Tchaikovsky', related the composer. 'I used to go out into the corridor and sit there for hours, the better to hear the music.' It is interesting to recall that in 1938, after the creation of the gigantic 5th Symphony, the composer tried to convey 'images of childhood — rather naive, bright, "spring-like" moods' in his first string quartet. Perhaps at that time there was a powerful association between the sound of that medium and his memories of childhood.

His father's singing, too, had a certain influence on the formation of the musical tastes of his childhood. Apart from the Gypsy songs that were then popular, young Dmitri became familiar through his father's singing, with Tchaikovsky's *Eugene Onegin* (his father no doubt made a very passable domestic Lensky), and an early revelation was a visit to the Opera to hear this same piece, with its wonderful lyrical roles, its captivating orchestration and its compassionate humanity. 'I knew much of the music by heart' Shostakovich told his friend and biographer Rabinovich:

But when I first heard the opera played by an orchestra I was amazed. A new world of orchestral music was unfolded before me, a world of new colours . . . '

The composer's admiration for Tchaikovsky continued into his adult composing life. Years later he had this to say about his music:

In development of musical idea and in orchestration he has no equal. I bow to his magnificent orchestration, for as a rule he did not orchestrate his compositions after they were written, as is usually done, but composed, as it were, *a priori,* for orchestra, *i.e.,* he thought in terms of orchestra. And whenever I myself encounter difficulty in the course of my work I invariably find the solution to my problem by studying Tchaikovsky's technique.

Eugene Onegin was young Dmitri's second memorable visit to the Opera. At the age of five he had been taken with his two sisters to hear Rimsky Korsakov's fairy tale opera 'Tsar Saltan', and it was after this experience that he entertained his family the next day with his own version of the opera in recitation and song. Such displays of precocious talent were not forced by his parents and he did not begin piano lessons with his mother until he was eight. Music was a normal part of family life (his elder sister had already begun piano lessons), and, in the eyes of his parents, a necessary part of their children's general education. Like all musical children with a creative gift, young Dmitri began to take pleasure in improvising at the piano as well as learning set pieces. His Aunt Nadejda recalled the first time he played for her:

Here is a snow-covered village far away' — a run and the beginning of a little tune accompanied his words — 'moonlight is shining on the empty road — here is a little house lit by a candle —' Mitya played his tune and then, looking slyly at his Aunt over the top of the piano, he suddenly flicked a note high in the treble — 'Somebody peeks in the window.'

Again, there would have been nothing remarkable about this in a childhood that was encouraged to take pleasure in inventive play rather than ready-made amusements. The children clearly enjoyed improvising their own family entertainment, and young Dmitri had displayed a penchant for dancing (the kopak was his favourite) and theatrical amusement. Books, theatre and music were all part of the cultured background in which Shostakovich grew up. (The fact that the young composer began to write his own first opera, *The Gypsies* after Pushkin, at the tender age of nine testifies to an early sophistication here).

First attempts at composition — the actual writing down of music — were persistent, despite a neutral, even sceptical, attitude towards this activity on the part of his parents. But as time went on it became evident that composition, no less than piano playing, was a commitment. Soon it was to be felt as a vocation.

In 1914 war with Germany broke out, but the family's domestic fortunes continued to rise. Dmitri père had acquired a position as Commercial Manager of an ammunition firm called Promet. They were now happily established in Nikolaevskaya Street and the family had moved into a new apartment — No. 9, fifth floor — across the street from a previous apartment at No. 16. The household had a country residence and two cars at their disposal. (Petersburg — now renamed Petrograd in the surge of anti German patriotic feeling — was then a city of a mere 2000 cars.) War hardly affected life in the Imperial City, which continued to display its pre-war glitter and splendour. Terrible losses were being suffered far away at the Front, and reports from the men there were disquieting — lack of equipment, food and ammunition, wastage of lives through incompetent leadership. But in spite

The composer Scriabin in 1914. His music was all the rage in St Petersburg (Novosti)

of this, and the now increasingly familiar sight of refugees and military hospitals, the social and artistic life of Petrograd was as full and exciting as ever. Famous names continued to appear at the Alexandrinka and Marinsky Theatre. Meyerhold was producing Shaw's *Pygmalion* and Wilde's *Picture of Dorian Gray*; the operas of Rimsky Korsakov, Mussorgsky, Borodin and Tchaikovsky (particularly *The Queen of Spades* and *Eugene Onegin*) were staged before enthusiastic audiences; symphony concerts by the Court

Orchestra were a regular feature (though composers with German names were being dropped from the programmes). 'But the real craze of the Petrograd musical world during the war,' wrote Alexander Werth was Scriabin. We young people used to regard him as a super-super Beethoven; and when we heard Kussevitsky conduct the *Poème de l'Extase*, we thought we had been present at one of the greatest events in the musical history of all time.

The war with Germany proved the last, fatal stress for the Tsar's government. We have already mentioned the massacre of 1912 at the Lena Gold Fields. The outbreak of war in 1914 had, in a first flush of patriotism, diverted attention from the country's plight — but as the war went on the gap between government and people became a yawning chasm. By the beginning of 1917 the people's disenchantment with a rapidly deteriorating state of affairs was complete. The only political party that opposed the war — the Bolsheviks, headed by Lenin in exile in Switzerland — was ignored and suppressed. The Duma, with little power of its own, continued to meet and hold its ineffectual debates. The Court had become the subject of scandal and disgust; Rasputin's hypnotic influence on the Tsarina and her Court was a despised symbol of the corruption and indolent power of Tsar Nicholas II. The strain of running the war was felt by all but the rich: hunger and reluctance to serve in an ill-equipped and badly run army brought to a head all the grievances of a people who had since 1905 never recovered their faith in Tsardom. Once again the city of Peter the Great became the arena for striking workers and mass demonstrations. But this time there was to be no going back: a whole era was to be swept away in a single year.

Chapter 4

The Year 1917

I don't want to be a wayside flower plucked after morning in an idle hour
Mayakovsky

In December 1916 Rasputin, the Tsarina's 'man of God' was murdered at a dinner party given by a group of noblemen and his body was thrown into the Neva. This was the first sign in Court circles of impatience with a corrupt administration. The Tsarina's heart was broken (she spent hours by his grave) but there was little

Bread queue in Petrograd, 1917 (Novosti)

Nevsky Prospekt, February 1917. A street meeting (Novosti)

sympathy for her bereavement outside the immediate family circle: there had been several plots to get rid of him before this successful one.

Early in 1917 the people of Petrograd began to take matters into their own hands. Food was scarce and bread rationing did nothing to improve the temper of the long queues of womenfolk — the wives and mothers of disgruntled soldiers at the Front or factory workers at home. In February strikes and street demonstrations broke out and, increasingly, serious casualties were inflicted on the populace by police and troops — whose allegiance to the Tsar, nevertheless, was already wavering. The tide of the people's revolution, unassisted at this stage by the professional revolutionaries, was gathering force. During these street riots young Dmitri witnessed a sight he never forgot.

> 'They were breaking up a crowd in the street' the composer recalled to Solomon Volkov, 'And a Cossack killed a boy with his sabre. It was terrifying. I ran home to tell my parents about it.'

So indelible was the impression that in two of his revolution-inspired symphonies (Nos. 2 and 12) this incident is described in

The beginning of Prokofiev's piano piece which captures the excitement of the crowd during the February Revolution. The music is marked 'Fast, agitated and very accented' (Reproduced by permission of Boosey & Hawkes Publishers Ltd.)

music. Caught up in all this excitement in the streets of revolutionary Petrograd was a young composer some fifteen years Dmitri's senior — Sergei Prokofiev.

'The February Revolution found me in Petrograd', he wrote. 'I and those I associated with welcomed it with open arms. I was in the streets of Petrograd while the fighting was going on, hiding behind house corners when the shooting came too close. No. 19 of the *Fugitive Visions* written at this time partly reflected my impression — the feeling of the crowd rather than the inner essence of the Revolution'.

On March 23rd a huge funeral procession took place in the city — soldiers, sailors, workers, students, marched down the Nevsky Prospekt to Mars Field where the bodies of those killed in the Revolution were to be buried in a common grave. They marched to the strains of the Revolutionary Funeral Hymn, *You fell as*

Victims, 'that slow, melancholy and yet triumphant chant, so Russian and so moving' as John Reed described it.

You fell in the fatal fight
For the liberty of the people, for the honour of the people.
You gave up your lives and everything dear to you,
You suffered in horrible prisons,
You went to exile in chains . . .
Without a word you carried your chains because you could not ignore your suffering brothers,
Because you believed that justice is stronger than the sword . . .
The time will come when your surrendered life will count.
The time is near; when tyranny falls the people will rise, great and free!
Farewell brothers, you chose a noble path,
At your grave we swear to fight, to work for freedom and the people's happiness . . .

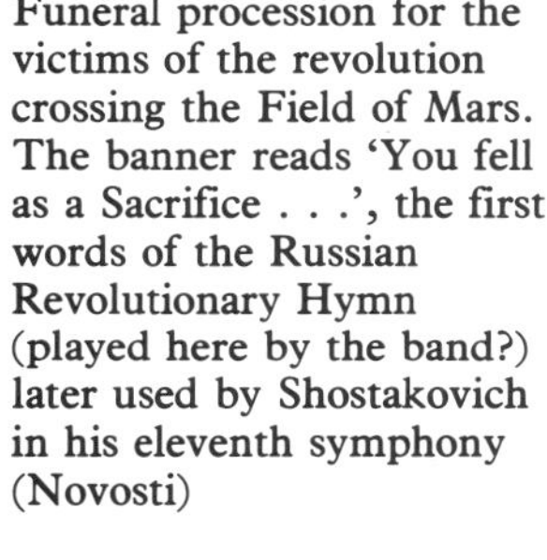

Petrograd, March 1917. Funeral procession for the victims of the revolution crossing the Field of Mars. The banner reads 'You fell as a Sacrifice . . .', the first words of the Russian Revolutionary Hymn (played here by the band?) later used by Shostakovich in his eleventh symphony (Novosti)

Young Mitya (which was Dmitri's nickname in the family) had been amongst the crowd that day with his parents and sisters. In the evening he sat down at the piano and played his 'Funeral March in Memory of the Victims of the Revolution' — a piece that came to be much in demand by visitors to the Shostakovich household.

'The Revolution, I'm convinced, was what made me into a composer,' Shostakovich said towards the end of his life, in a conversation with the Television Producer Ian Engelmann.

That may be putting it too sweepingly, perhaps, but that was when I first felt a vocation for composition . . . of course I was very young in 1917, but my first childish compositions were dedicated to the Revolution and inspired by it. I wrote a sort of wordless Revolution Hymn, then a Funeral March in memory of the victims of the Revolution, and then an unfinished work I called Revolutionary Petrograd. I resurrected the title for one of the movements of my twelfth symphony . . .'

Pasternak's hero, Yury, in his novel *Dr. Zhivago* spoke for his time in these words: 'Revolution erupted forcibly like a breath held too long. Everyone revived, became transformed, transfigured, changed. Everyone seemed to experience two such upheavals, his own personal revolution and a second one common to all.'

In the face of massive popular demonstrations the Tsar was forced to abdicate. A 'dual power' (in Lenin's phrase) consisting of a Provisional Government (drawn mainly from the Liberal and Conservative leaders) and 'Soviets' (or workers' and soldiers' councils) was formed to replace the toppled Imperial Government. While both sides of this dual interregnum needed, but mistrusted each other, they were nevertheless united in a fear of the monarchist army officers who might seek to restore the Tsarist régime. In the Soviet's famous 'Order No. 1' the soldiers were called upon to ignore their officers and elect their own regimental committees.

And now Lenin — Russia's most famous professional revolutionary — joined the struggle for power in Petrograd. (Lenin's real name was Vladmir Ulyanov. His revolutionary name 'Lenin' derived from the river Lena in Siberia — the place of penal servitude where he and his fellow conspirators had been schooled.) It was the German authorities who provided the Bolshevik leader in exile in Zürich with the means to return to Petrograd, because they knew that his opposition to the war would divide the dual power and weaken the Russian war effort still further. His arrival in a sealed train at the Finland Station in April 1917 (young Mitya tagged along with some school friends to join the crowd) with his harsh call for 'All land to the Peasants' and 'No more war' gained immediate popular support. Demonstrations against the Provisional Government soon followed. But Lenin's 'Peace and Bread' cry had its strong opponents in the government, who were committed to other priorities, including the prosecution of the war with Germany. They were able to appeal to a spirit of war patriotism in branding Lenin as a German agent and issued a warrant for his arrest. Lenin was forced into hiding. At Razliv,

Lenin speaks in the Tauride Palace on his return to Petrograd, April, 1917 (SCR)

near Sestrovetsk, where he lived in a hut, he disguised himself in a wig and make-up to resemble a workman, by means of which he procured a passport photograph to travel to Finland. There he waited in some impatience for events to take their course, brooding over the responsibility of power that was at last within his grasp after years of waiting in exile. This is the inspiration of the second movement of Shostakovich's 12th symphony, which takes its name from Lenin's Razliv retreat. As Lenin's widow, in her reminiscences, put it,

> His mind was constantly engaged in the problem of how to re-organise the whole State apparatus, how the masses were to be re-organised, how the whole social fabric was to be re-woven — as he expressed it.

Revolutionary Petrograd, 1917. The shooting of the July demonstrators by troops of the Provisional Government in the Nevsky Prospekt. Such scenes, which the young Shostakovich lived through, inspired the first movement of his twelfth symphony (Novosti)

Meanwhile in Petrograd Lenin's Bolshevik Party was earning the title of 'Saviours of the Revolution', to the dismay of the increasingly unpopular Provisional Government led by Kerensky who insisted on pressing ahead with the war against Germany before attending to internal reforms. A Russian General with Napoleonic ambitions named Kornilov, who had marched with troops against the city intending to restore law and order in a military coup, was completely frustrated and dispelled by a force of citizens largely organised by the Bolsheviks. Shortly after this, Lenin's old political rival and new comrade in arms, Leon Trotsky, was released from prison and through his persuasive oratory and organising skill was able to build up the military power of the Red Guard — the Bolshevik's own illegal army. A Military Revolutionary Committee was formed, and Lenin (still in risk of arrest) travelled in disguise to the Bolshevik Headquarters at the Smolny Institute, there to take his place at the centre of activities. The plan was to seize power from Kerensky's government by a show of force, key points in the city having been already occupied by the Red Guards. Trotsky, in his colourful, romantic style describes the atmosphere of the deciding night in Petrograd, 25th–26th October, which he and Lenin passed together in trying to snatch some sleep on the floor of a room at the Smolny Institute:

Lenin disguised in wig and make-up for his forged passport photograph (SCR)

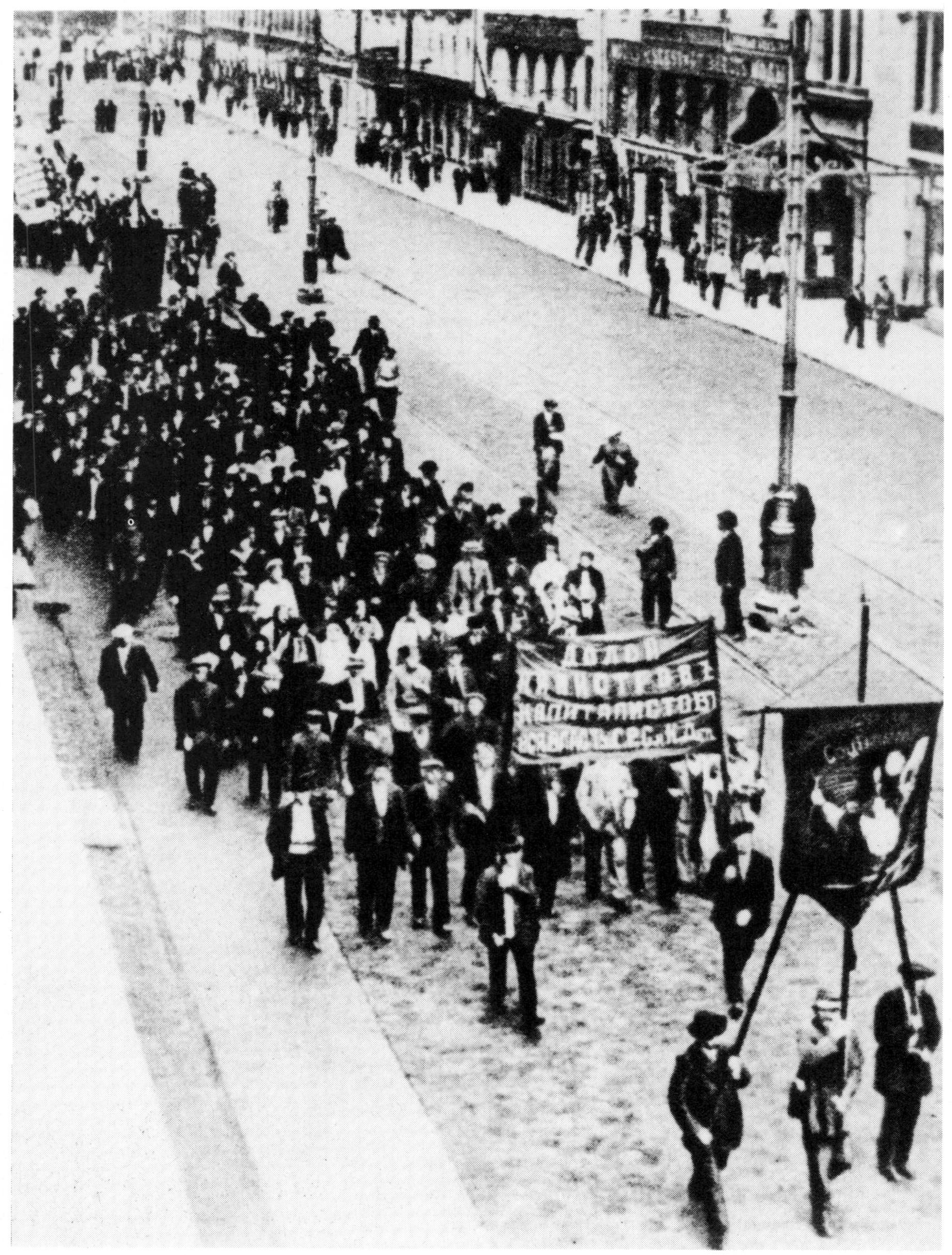

The July Demonstration. Workers in the city carry the slogans 'Down with the War!', 'Down with the Capitalist Ministers', 'All Power to the Soviets'. (Novosti)

One can readily picture the deserted streets of Petrograd, dimly lit, and whipped by the autumn winds from the sea; the bourgeois and officials cowering in their beds, trying to guess what is going on in those dangerous and mysterious streets; the workers' quarters quiet with the tense sleep of a war-camp. Commissions and conferences of the government parties are exhausting themselves in impotence in the Tsar's palaces, where the living ghosts of democracy rub shoulders with the still hovering ghosts of the monarchy. Now and again the silks and gildings of the halls are plunged into darkness — the supplies of coal have run short. In the various districts detachments of workers, soldiers, and sailors are keeping watch. The young proletarians have rifles and machine-gun belts across their shoulders. Street pickets are warming themselves at fires in the streets. The life of the capital, thrusting its head from one epoch into another on this autumn night, is concentrated about a group of telephones.

The next morning the Military Revolutionary Committee proclaimed the revolution victorious. By the afternoon the Winter Palace, seat of the Kerensky government, was surrounded. After a

The Battleship *Aurora* in 1917 (Novosti)

Декретъ о мирѣ,

принятый единогласно на засѣданіи Всероссійскаго Съѣзда Совѣтовъ Рабочихъ, Солдатскихъ и Крестьянскихъ Депутатовъ 26 октября 1917 г.

Рабочее и крестьянское правительство, созданное революціей 24—25 октября и опирающееся на Совѣты Рабочихъ, Солдатскихъ и Крестьянскихъ Депутатовъ, предлагаетъ всѣмъ воюющимъ народамъ и ихъ правительствамъ начать немедленно переговоры о справедливомъ демократическомъ мирѣ.

Справедливымъ или демократическимъ миромъ, котораго жаждетъ подавляющее большинство истощенныхъ, измученныхъ и истерзанныхъ войной рабочихъ и трудящихся классовъ всѣхъ воюющихъ странъ,—миромъ, котораго самымъ опредѣленнымъ и настойчивымъ образомъ требовали русскіе рабочіе и крестьяне послѣ сверженія царской монархіи,—такимъ миромъ правительство считаетъ немедленный миръ безъ аннексій (т. е. безъ захвата чужихъ земель, безъ насильственнаго присоединенія чужихъ народностей) и безъ контрибуцій.

Такой миръ предлагаетъ Правительство Россіи заключить всѣмъ воюющимъ народамъ немедленно, выражая готовность сдѣлать безъ малѣйшей оттяжки тотчасъ-же всѣ рѣшительные шаги впредь до окончательнаго утвержденія всѣхъ условій такого мира полномочными собраніями народныхъ представителей всѣхъ странъ и всѣхъ націй.

Подъ аннексіей или захватомъ чужихъ земель Правительство понимаетъ сообразно правовому сознанію демократіи вообще, и трудящихся классовъ въ особенности, всякое присоединеніе къ большому или сильному государству малой или слабой народности безъ точно, ясно и добровольно выраженнаго согласія и желанія этой народности, независимо отъ того, когда это насильственное присоединеніе совершено, независимо также отъ того, насколько развитой или отсталой является насильственно присоединяемая или насильственно удерживаемая въ границахъ даннаго государства нація. Независимо, наконецъ, отъ того, въ Европѣ или въ далекихъ заокеанскихъ странахъ эта нація живетъ.

Если какая бы то ни была нація удерживается въ границахъ даннаго государства насиліемъ, если ей, вопреки выраженному съ ея стороны желанію—все равно, выражено ли это желаніе въ печати, въ народныхъ собраніяхъ, въ рѣшеніяхъ партій или возмущеніяхъ и возстаніяхъ противъ національнаго гнета—не предоставляется права свободнымъ голосованіемъ, при полномъ выводѣ войска присоединяющей или вообще болѣе сильной націи, рѣшить безъ малѣйшаго принужденія вопросъ о формахъ государственнаго существованія этой націи, то присоединеніе ея является аннексіей, т. е. захватомъ и насиліемъ.

Продолжать эту войну изъ-за того, какъ раздѣлить между сильными и богатыми націями захваченныя ими слабыя народности, Правительство считаетъ величайшимъ преступленіемъ противъ человѣчества и торжественно заявляетъ свою рѣшимость немедленно подписать условія мира, прекращающаго эту войну на указанныхъ, равно справедливыхъ для всѣхъ безъ изъятія народностей условіяхъ.

Вмѣстѣ съ тѣмъ Правительство заявляетъ, что оно отнюдь не считаетъ вышеуказанныхъ условій мира ультимативными, т. е. соглашается разсмотрѣть и всякія другія условія мира, настаивая лишь на возможно болѣе быстромъ предложеніи ихъ какой бы то ни было воюющей страной и на полнѣйшей ясности, на безусловномъ исключеніи всякой двусмысленности и всякой тайны при предложеніи условій мира.

Тайную дипломатію Правительство отмѣняетъ, со своей стороны выражая твердое намѣреніе вести всѣ переговоры совершенно открыто передъ всѣмъ народомъ, приступая немедленно къ полному опубликованію тайныхъ договоровъ, подтвержденныхъ или заключенныхъ правительствомъ помѣщиковъ и капиталистовъ съ февраля по 25 октября 1917 года. Все содержаніе этихъ тайныхъ договоровъ, поскольку оно направлено, какъ это въ большинствѣ случаевъ бывало, къ доставленію выгодъ и привилегій русскимъ помѣщикамъ и капиталистамъ, къ удержанію или увеличенію аннексій великороссовъ, Правительство объявляетъ безусловно и немедленно отмѣненнымъ.

Обращаясь съ предложеніемъ къ правительствамъ и народамъ всѣхъ странъ начать немедленно открытые переговоры о заключеніи мира, Правительство выражаетъ съ своей стороны готовность вести эти переговоры, какъ посредствомъ письменныхъ сношеній, по телеграфу, такъ и путемъ переговоровъ между представителями разныхъ странъ или на конференціи таковыхъ представителей. Для облегченія такихъ переговоровъ Правительство назначаетъ своего полномочнаго представителя въ нейтральныя страны.

Правительство предлагаетъ всѣмъ правительствамъ и народамъ всѣхъ воюющихъ странъ немедленно заключить перемиріе, причемъ со своей стороны считаетъ желательнымъ, чтобы это перемиріе было заключено не меньше, какъ на три мѣсяца, т. е. на такой срокъ, въ теченіе котораго вполнѣ возможно, какъ завершеніе переговоровъ о мирѣ съ участіемъ представителей всѣхъ безъ изъятія народностей или націй, втянутыхъ въ войну или вынужденныхъ къ участію въ ней, такъ равно и созывъ полномочныхъ собраній народныхъ представителей всѣхъ странъ для окончательнаго утвержденія условій мира.

Обращаясь съ этимъ предложеніемъ мира къ правительствамъ и народамъ всѣхъ воюющихъ странъ, временное рабочее и крестьянское правительство Россіи обращается также въ особенности къ сознательнымъ рабочимъ трехъ самыхъ передовыхъ націй человѣчества и самыхъ крупныхъ участвующихъ въ настоящей войнѣ государствъ, Англіи, Франціи и Германіи. Рабочіе этихъ странъ оказали наибольшія услуги дѣлу прогресса и соціализма и великіе образцы чартистскаго движенія въ Англіи, рядъ революцій, имѣвшихъ всемірно-историческое значеніе, совершенныхъ французскимъ пролетаріатомъ, наконецъ, въ геройской борьбѣ противъ исключительнаго закона въ Германіи и образцовой для рабочихъ всего міра длительной, упорной дисциплинированной работѣ созданія массовыхъ пролетарскихъ организацій Германіи. Всѣ эти образцы пролетарскаго героизма и историческаго творчества служатъ намъ порукой за то, что рабочіе названныхъ странъ поймутъ лежащія на нихъ теперь задачи освобожденія человѣчества отъ ужасовъ войны и ея послѣдствій, что эти рабочіе всесторонней рѣшительной и беззавѣтно энергичной дѣятельностью своей помогутъ намъ успѣшно довести до конца дѣло мира и вмѣстѣ съ тѣмъ дѣло освобожденія трудящихся и эксплоатируемыхъ массъ населенія отъ всякаго рабства и всякой эксплоатаціи.

(Гл. V, стр. 117)

Lenin's Decree on Peace, 26th October, 1917 (SCR)

somewhat unco-ordinated military operation which lasted until nightfall, with few casualties, the storming was complete. Kerensky's government surrendered without resistance: suddenly Lenin and Trotsky found themselves in power, though bitter struggles lay ahead.

In his symphony about the year 1917, Shostakovich gave his third movement the title 'Aurora', after the cruiser whose guns signalled the historic attack on the Winter Palace. (The old battleship, moored on the Neva in its original revolutionary position, is a familiar sight to Leningraders, as, of course, it was to Shostakovich himself as a boy.) The heroic, Beethovenian rhetoric of that movement presents, perhaps, a somewhat idealised portrait of what was, in reality, a rather amateurish military operation. But the gun salvo, so excitingly thundered out in Shostakovich's symphony, truly heralded 'The Dawn of Humanity' for the Russian people. The Soviet Union had been born. To a schoolboy of eleven who lived through that day within earshot of the Aurora's guns it cannot have failed to be an inspiration.

Chapter 5

Schoolboy, Piano Student and Rising Young Composer (1917–1923)

When the revolution began in February 1917 Dmitri was in his first year at school — at the Shidlovskaya Gymnasium, one of the many institutions which had sprung up since 1905 for the education of the sons of the liberal intelligentsia. At the same time he was a pupil at Herr Ignatiy Albertovich Gliasser's Music School where, following a year's private tuition from his mother, he had been sent in 1915 for the further development of his talent. Here, until 1919, he learnt the piano with Herr Gliasser's wife, and then with Herr Gliasser himself. He rapidly distinguished himself, receiving every encouragement at home from his parents, and from his mother in particular who kept a watchful eye on his progress. Despite the turbulent political events of the time — the abdication of the Tsar on 3rd March, the uncertainty of the eight months of Provisional Government, Lenin's October coup and

The young Mitya (front row — second from right) as a pupil at Gliassers Music School, 1918. Herr Gliasser sits in the middle, arms folded (Novosti)

Kustodiev's portrait of the 13 year old Mitya in 1919 (Novosti)

the proclamation of 'All power to the Soviets' — the childrens' musical and general education continued undisturbed. One of young Dmitri's first public performances at Gliasser's — at a concert given by the pupils in 1917 — was of Handel's *Largo*. It is a little odd to imagine a composer as intensely Russian as Shostakovich playing Handel's bland air which has, in this country, acquired almost institutional overtones. But so it was, and his audience sat entranced at the musical concentration and projection of this performance by the young pupil in his sailor jacket and long trousers. At Gliasser's he learnt to play Bach's *48*, was discovered to have a good musical memory and an excellent ear. The *48*, in which Beethoven, Chopin and Schumann had been schooled, were to remain an inspiration long into the composer's adult life — indeed, his whole piano study was in the Central European tradition of what Busoni had called 'the three B's' — Bach, Beethoven and Brahms — all of them important historical influences on Shostakovich's composing. (He was, after hearing a performance of Bach's *48* in 1952 to write his own two books of Preludes and Fugues.) Of Gliasser himself Shostakovich seems to have entertained little respect. 'A very self confident but dull man' he reported to Solomon Volkov 'And his lectures always seemed ridiculous to me.'

In 1919 it was decided to send Dmitri to the children's classes at the Conservatoire which, while not interfering with the boy's regular schooling, would bring him into contact with an altogether more professionally orientated musical environment. A fine portrait of the young musician dates from this time inscribed 'To my young friend Mitya Shostakovich, September 1919'. It is by B. M. Kustodiev, a well known painter, illustrator and theatre designer of his day, an invalid who was already doomed to spend the rest of his short life in a wheel chair. In May of the following year Kustodiev portrayed the young musician at the piano. An actor at the Malyi Theatre, one Zhuravlev, recalled on television how Kustodiev came to meet the boy. Campbell Creighton, who watched the programme, reported Zhuravlev's anecdote as follows:

> One of Mitya's schoolfellows was the daughter of a Petrograd artist, one day she told her father that there was a boy in their class who was 'absolutely fab' on the piano: could she invite him home? He came to tea and was duly asked to play, which he did: Chopin, Beethoven, etc., until the girl interrupted him, asking why he was playing that old classical stuff, and begging him to play a foxtrot. Papa rebuked her, and said to young Shostakovich: 'Mitya, don't pay any attention to her. Play what you want to play.' And continued with his sketch.

Kustodiev was a great lover of music and the young pianist spent

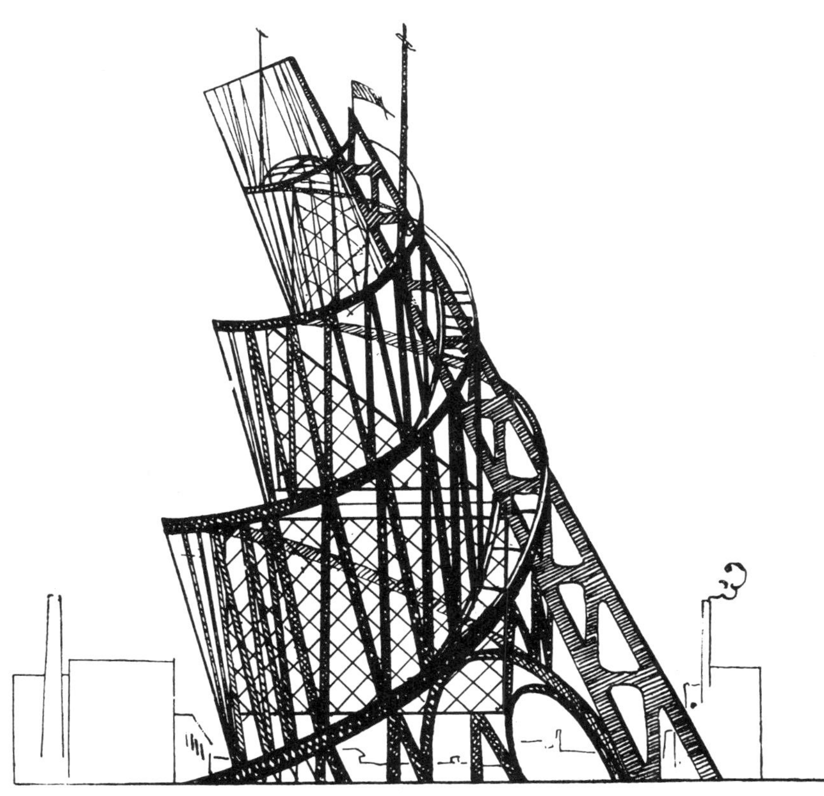

Tatlin's design for a monument to the Third International in 1920. (The design, to be constructed out of iron and glass and erected in Moscow, was not executed.) The spiral became a symbol in Russian revolutionary art, and Shostakovich's revolution-inspired music was influenced by the image. (SCR)

many hours playing to him. (Later he dedicated the first of a set of early Preludes, Op.2, to him.) Towards the end of his life Shostakovich recalled how, when afflicted with pain, Kustodiev's face would divide into two — one half red, the other half white — and how he learnt many things about art and Russian painters from him. One should remember that this period was a vital one in the history of Russian art, which was, internationally, very 'advanced'. The movement known as Constructivism — with which the composer himself was later to be briefly involved — was just beginning to assert its claim on the attention of a young post-revolutionary generation. The old conception of art as entertainment, as expensive property to be purchased and consumed by the aristocratic few, was under attack. Art now had to have a social, contemporary relevance, drawing on new images for its inspiration. 'The art of the future' wrote Rodchenko in 1920 'will not be the cosy decoration of family homes. It will be just as indispensable as 48 storey sky scrapers, mighty bridges, wireless, aeronautics and submarines which will be transformed into art.' Kustodiev, who was just over forty at this time and a painter in the old representational tradition, would have been out of sympathy with this radical view but can hardly have failed to mention these developments to his young sitter. The portrait remained a favourite of Shostakovich, hanging in his Moscow flat up to the time of his death.

The alert, humorous boy of Kustodiev's portrait, with his sensitive mouth and serious attitude to music, was quickly noticed by Glazunov, the composer-director of the Conservatoire. After hearing some piano music composed by Dmitri at that time he advised him to study composition there as well as piano. Dmitri became a pupil of Maximilian Steinberg, son-in-law of Rimsky Korsakov, who had been Glazunov's predecessor. Glazunov took great interest in the boy, behaving towards him with fatherly concern after the sudden death of Dmitri Boleslavovich of a heart

A Russian Civil War Poster, 1920: 'Have you Volunteered?'. Note the slogan at the top right corner 'Proletarians of your Country, Unite' — a Soviet adaptation of the closing words of Karl Marx's Communist Manifesto, 1848 (SCR)

ailment in 1922. Life was now very different from the former prosperous, pre-revolutionary days for the Shostakovich family. It is more than likely that the father's death was accelerated by the strains, financial, material and social, of coming to terms with the new régime and the aftermath of revolution. Lenin's political coup of October 1917 had been followed by three years of Civil War, and during this period the civilian population suffered terribly from lack of food and fuel in the bitter winter periods. The poetess Akhmatova recorded in her diary that Petersburg had turned into the diametrical opposite of itself, 'what with typhus, famine, shootings, apartments plunged into darkness and people so swollen from famine as to be unrecognisable . . .' The passing of the old order had to be accepted. The brutal murder of the Tsar's family at Yekaterinburg in July 1918 (regarded by Lenin and Trotsky as a necessary sacrifice) was said to have precipitated the slide into Civil War; Petrograd lost its status as capital city, giving way to Moscow as the seat of Government; the country now adopted the Gregorian calendar, doing away with the previous Julian calendar thirteen day time lag; Lenin's 'War Communism' involved the complete nationalisation of industry and commerce, compulsory levies of food stuffs from the peasants, payments in kind for workers and the imposition of compulsory labour on the bourgeoisie. A rather sad story of the commandeering of the Shostakovich family car by soldiers of the revolution, and of the quiet dignity of Sophia's surrender to the demand, no more than hints at the adjustments the family had to make as the revolution began to bite into their domestic circumstances. For a man like Dmitri's father, who had witnessed in the years before his death the sharp decline of 'bourgeois' values that he himself had lived by, it must have been a harsh time. It is one thing to accept in principle the need for a social revolution, (after all, the liberal intelligentsia had sought change for decades), it is another thing to adjust to its physical realities if your own lot has been comfortable. The Shostakovich family, with a summer residence at the Rennenkampf Estate, servants and a company car at their disposal, had enjoyed a standard of living which was to disappear after the father's death.

Dmitri *père* had been a devoted family man. His work never seemed to encroach on his life with his family with whom he shared his passion for gadgets, wire and ring puzzles, solitaire and music. Shostakovich's last symphony begins with a 'toyshop' movement which could well hark back to the days he and his two sisters spent with their father engrossed in mechanical amusements; and as for puzzles, the more one gets to know the 'private' music of the string quartets the more one senses that the composer delighted in pitting his own musical wits against his listeners in the constant game of hide and seek he plays with his themes. Perhaps much of the composer's playful side came from his father; his mother was made of sterner stuff — her stoicism and seriousness, coupled with determination and ambition to do the best she could for her three children, were to be the mainstay of the family during the difficult days ahead. On her husband's death she took up a post as typist at the Chamber of Weights and Measures, and her sister Nadejda and her husband moved into the Shostakovich apartment in support of the bereaved family.

As for the young Shostakovich's own development at the Conservatoire, he was, as yet, no revolutionary in music, however closely he identified with the spirit of the Russian Revolution. Glazunov's dislike of 'harmful trends' in music had already found

The Leningrad State Conservatory. Rimsky Korsakov's statue in the foreground (SCR)

Glazunov, Shostakovich's guide and mentor after the death of his father (Walter Lemberg, Talinn)

expression in 1914 when he spoke against the young Prokofiev winning first prize in piano playing with his first concerto. With Glazunov's special interest in the boy, there would have been no encouragement of anything experimental at such a tender age. (Two of the most ardent revolutionary spirits in Russian music, Stravinsky and Prokofiev, had already left the country. And as for Scriabin, who had died in 1915, his music was considered 'decadent' in leading Conservatoire circles.) In any case, piano and composition were on equal footing: there was every possibility that Dmitri was heading for a career on the concert platform. ('After finishing at the Conservatoire I was confronted with the problem — should I become a pianist or a composer?' Shostakovich recalled. 'The latter won. If the truth be told I should have been both, but it's too late now to blame myself for such a ruthless decision.')

The year his father died, Dmitri, on the advice of Glazunov, left school and became a full time music student at the Conservatoire. He now studied piano with Leonid Nikolayev and continued his composition sessions with Maximilian Steinberg. (At the Conser-

L. Nikolayev, Shostakovich's piano teacher at the Conservatoire (Novosti)

vatoire this meant the disciplines of harmony, counterpoint, fugue and orchestration.) But if the Volkov memoirs are to be believed, it was Glazunov who most excited the young musician's admiration. The quality of Glazunov's ear, his insistence on solid, impeccable craftsmanship, his astonishing memory for all music, including individual work of his students — all these things made a lasting impression, and contributed to the making of Shostakovich's impeccable professionalism. Nikolayev was a teacher of great repute — Head of Piano Studies at the Conservatoire. The lasting esteem in which Dmitri held him can be gauged by the fact that Shostakovich's second piano sonata (first performed by the composer in Moscow in 1943) was dedicated to his memory when he died in 1942. It is important to remember that Shostakovich's musical training as a composer was in the classical tradition — keyboard based, with a strong sense of the relationship between composer and performer, and a Brahmsian belief in the capacity of an orchestral work to be tested in black and white at the piano. Nowadays it is less frequent for a composer to be a fine performer, but musicians overlapping with Shostakovich's generation — Bartok, Britten and Hindemith among them — were all fine executant composers.

All his life the piano figured in his compositions — the first, fifth and seventh symphonies all contain important parts for the instrument — and although his interest in the piano as a solo instument declined in later years he wrote a succession of fine chamber works for strings and piano, including his last completed compositon, the viola sonata.

His interest in the piano sonatas of Beethoven was a formative influence on him from student days onwards and his graduation recital of 1923 included the *Appassionata* sonata. He also studied Beethoven's *Hammerklavier* sonata, a formidable challenge to technique and musical understanding. Thus at an early age we may observe Shostakovich's pre-occupation with music of an earlier revolutionary era in Europe, and his interpretative identification with the music of Beethoven became no less a creative one as, in later years, he emerged as a kind of Soviet Beethoven, composing music on the same heroic scale as his historic predecessor.

Beethoven, was a figure of special historic importance to the Soviet ideologists of Shostakovich's youth. Said to be Lenin's favourite composer, Beethoven was held up as a supreme example of a creative artist whose message was in tune with the social aspirations of his age. The symphony in Europe, for example, was held to have been in decline since Beethoven, because capitalist society made it increasingly impossible to uphold the idea of the brotherhood of man which Beethoven, in his ninth symphony, so

Beethoven. An imaginary portrait by L. Pasternak (father of the poet) in 1920. 'The idolization of Beethoven as a revolutionary hero became a Soviet obsession, stimulated by Lunacharsky, Asafiev and many other authors.' Boris Schwarz

inspiringly celebrated. Symphonic composers of nineteenth century Europe were considered to have withdrawn into a dreamy and isolated individualism. Mahler and his music, always popular in Russia, was thought to express a sharp awareness of the cleavage between fine, humanistic ideals and the impossibility of their realisation in a capitalist age. Perhaps a new symphonic composer in the Beethoven tradition would arise in Soviet Russia? As it turned out, this was to become Shostakovich's official role, and that he was well fitted for it was to be revealed in his own first symphony, a work whose slow movement and finale displayed a rhetorical power that went straight back to the example of Beethoven and Mahler. Boris Schwarz has written about

> Russia's unique attitude towards Beethoven which is admiring and possessive. Already in the nineteenth century, Russian musicians were absorbed by Beethoven studies. This idolization of Beethoven as a revolutionary hero became a Soviet obsession, stimulated by Lunacharsky, Asafiev and many other authors . . .

Young Shostakovich, in addition to acquiring a reputation in the performance of Beethoven, was busy playing his own compositions and was already known to the Petrograd audiences. One of his first reviews published in the journal *Zhizn Iskusstva* (Art Life) in 1923 had this to say about his performance:

> The concert of the young pianist-composer Dmitri Shostakovich made an excellent impression. He played the Bach Organ Prelude and Fugue in A minor in the Liszt transcription, Beethoven's Appassionata Sonata, and his own works — all with a clarity of artistic intention that showed him to be a musician who deeply feels and understands his art. Shostakovich's compositions, his Variations, Preludes and Fantastic Dances, are fine examples of serious musical thought.

He was on the threshhold of a breakthrough to international acclaim for a student chef d'oeuvre without parallel in the history of music — the first symphony.

Chapter 6

The First Symphony
International Acclaim for a Soviet Genius (1924–1927)

The Revolution had to be implemented — socially, politically and institutionally. The Nikolaevskaya Street of our young composer's childhood now had its old name changed to Marat Street (after the French Revolutionist — history provided the early

Stalin and Kirov in Leningrad, 1926. Kirov, assassinated in December 1934, was an early victim of Stalin's political purges. (SCR)

Stalin and Lenin (SCR)

Soviet régime with plenty of such readymade substitues). After Lenin's death Petrograd was renamed Leningrad in honour of the great leader. Lenin, the architect of the Revolution, had died after a second stroke in January 1924 at the age of 53, and Stalin (who was responsible for the new State's collective title of USSR) was emerging as his likely — and feared — successor. (Stalin's real name was Joseph Vissarionovich Dzhugashvili; as a revolutionary he adopted the name of 'stal' or steel.) His rise was to mean political extermination for Lenin's close colleague, Leon Trotsky, and with him a host of other 'undesirable' elements — real or imagined — who seemed to pose a threat to Stalin's dictatorship. An era of liberal, civilized values was coming to an end and many artists and intellectuals were to suffer for their talent. The Civil War was now over, and Russia had entered the period of the New Economic Policy inaugurated by Lenin in 1921 as a means of rebuilding the country's shattered economy through limited free trade — a concession towards the peasants who had remained antagonistic to Lenin's political coup. Pasternak called the New Economic policy 'the most false and ambiguous of all Soviet

ЛЕНИНГРАДСКОЕ ОБЩЕСТВО
СМЫЧКИ ГОРОДА С ДЕРЕВНЕЙ.

Установить общение между городом и деревней, одна из основных задач рабочего класса, стоящего у власти.

В. И. ЛЕНИН.

'Union between Town and Country'. Society of Leningrad, 1925. A poster by Kustodiev, who knew Shostakovich well and made two famous portraits of the young composer (see page 55). The poster dates from the period of the New Economic Policy inaugurated by Lenin to win over the Peasants to the Soviet cause. The slogan below is a quotation from Lenin: 'One of the fundamental tasks of a working class which is worthy of power is to establish a bond between town and country'. (SCR)

periods'. Die-hard revolutionaries saw it as a betrayal of the original Communist ideal. Amongst them was Mayakovsky, who later wrote a play on 'Nepman mentality' (for which Shostakovich supplied music which was required to sound like 'a local fireman's band') called *The Bedbug*. Others, less politically minded, welcomed the New Economic Policy as a relief from the harshness and rigours of war. The writer Zamyatin recalled that 'The recently boarded up shop windows once again glittered with lights . . . Cafes and restaurants dotted the streets. Instead of machine-gun fire, the streets resounded with the hammering of boiler makers, bricklayers and carpenters'. Orthodox religion was a despised part of the old régime which had to be done away with. 'Neither Sorcerer, nor God nor servants of God are a help to us' wrote Mayakovsky in one of his exhortatory cartoons. The world had to be rebuilt without the help of religion which Karl Marx had branded as 'the opium of the people'.

For young Dmitri and the fatherless family of mother and daughters it was a period of worry, material hardship and hard work. He had by now finished his course in piano playing at the Conservatoire, though piano studies with Nikolayev on a more or less unofficial basis continued until he left in 1926. After his grounding in the theoretical diciplines of composition, he was now required to spend a further two years in 'free' composition, though of course he had been composing 'freely' (unofficially, so to speak) ever since 1917. His life at home and his position as a student at the Conservatoire were far from easy. The impoverished family were reduced to selling anything for food, expenses for medical treatment had to be met (both Dmitri and his mother were often ill during this time) and with his mother out of work it fell to the lot of the three younger members of the family to do what they could. Marusia, the elder sister who was twenty-one, got a job as a music teacher in a ballet school and gave some piano lessons. Dmitri, to the horror of his mother, found part time employment as a piano player for silent Movies at the 'Bright Reel' Theatre.

'My memories of the Bright Reel' he related to Volkov 'are not the most pleasant ones . . . My work consisted in providing musical accompaniments for the human passions on the screen. It was disgusting and exhausting. Hard work and low pay. But I put up with it and looked forward to receiving even that paltry sum. That's how hard up we were then.'

Pounding away on an out-of-tune upright piano in the draughty, smelly theatre, Dmitri would work away until late at night and arrive home exhausted around 1.00 a.m. Zoya, the younger sister, a sixteen year old high school girl, was the despair of her mother — she was (according to her aunt) the rebel of the family, and rather resented for not pulling her weight by both her elder sister and brother. Sophia, as a widow and mother, went through an appalling time. This highly educated and cultured woman, now in her late forties, had been reduced to working thirteen hours a day as cashier in the Workers' Union in order to support her family. There she became suspected of dishonesty after the disappearance of 100 roubles from her cash desk — and was dismissed her post. Prior to losing her job she had been robbed and badly wounded in the head one night by an attacker who thought she might have been carrying money as she returned from work. Small wonder that she felt her life was finished. But her physical resilience and determination saw her through (she was, in fact, to live for another twenty years) and her belief in her son's talent, her dedication to the task of helping him at the outset of his career, strengthened her resolve to do her duty as a mother.

There can be little doubt that the family's 'bourgeois' background was no help to them in those treacherous times. The Working Class and Working Class Culture were now taking over with a vengeance: the old bourgeois intelligentsia were hard hit.

The 'Bright Reel' Cinema in Leningrad (now called 'The Barricade') where the young Shostakovich played for silent films to supplement the family income. (Drawing by David Cook after a photograph)

Soviet Movie Posters at the time the young Shostakovich played for silent films (SCR)

With jobs difficult to come by, Madam Shostakovich, with her well-to-do family connections and educational privilege of a discredited era, would have been amongst the first to suffer in such a state of affairs. Dislike of the bourgeoisie extended to its artifacts. Contempt for the values of pre-revolutionary art was manifest everywhere. Groups were springing up that sought to replace the art of the past with something 'new' or — what could be even worse — 'non-élitist' in character, and this presented a real threat to the survival of the best. Lenin had been a bulwark against philistinism. 'We must preserve the beautiful, take it as a starting point, even if it is "old", he had proclaimed. 'Why must we bow low in front of the new, as if it were God, only because it is "new"?'

The brash dogmas and noisy polemics of literary and artistic cliques had their counterpart in music. In 1923 a group was formed called 'The Association of Proletarian Musicians' which in their publications cast aspersions on both the music of the past and certain respected living composers as 'alien' to proletarian aspiration. Although Lenin's enlightened Minister of Culture, Anatole Lunacharsky, was not impressed with such nonsense, these ideas began to invade the Conservatoires, so that there was in certain circles criticism of music which was 'technically skilful in form, but in content expressing the ideology of decadent bourgeoisie'. In the face of a lowering of standards (there was considerable pressure on the Conservatoire to lower its admission requirements) it became necessary to speak out in defence of 'old' culture.

'There is Glazunov, hence there is Russian music', Asafiev (a prominent critic and academic) had said, but Glazunov's influence as composer and administrator was on the wane.

Essentially part of the old liberal culture in music, he was, in fact, to leave the country for Paris in 1928.

In such a climate of opinion, with politics invading the Conservatoires, the young Shostakovich did not escape jealousy and intrigue. He had enjoyed Glazunov's personal patronage ever since the death of his father, but there are signs that during his post-graduate years as a composition student his position became insecure as a result of the increased political power of the student body.

According to Seroff:

> A group of students headed by two whose names were Schmidt and Renzin had voted Mitya out of the Academy and he was officially considered expelled from his piano class at the Conservatory. The same group of students with the backing of the authorities wanted to suspend the scholarship given by Glazunov, of eight roubles each winter month, but Glazunov, since it was a gift in his own name, prevented this.

Another Conservatoire intrigue prevented him from securing the official backing of Nikolayev for a scheduled performance of Tchaikovsky's first piano concerto. Such frustrations cannot have improved Dmitri's physically low condition or sweetened his outlook on life, but there is evidence to suggest that he made the most of his time. In addition to hearing and playing a lot of music (and Leningrad had much to offer in the way of novelties from abroad at this time for the young and adventurous) he read widely in Russian literature (Gogol and Blok were amongst his favourites) and professed an admiration for the genius of Shakespeare and Byron.

In the autumn of 1924 he began work on his student magnum opus — the first symphony — under the supervision of Steinberg, who saw to it that it was polished in the best traditions of Conservatoire craftsmanship.

In its firmness of structure, its thematic integration, its balance of forms and its assured instrumentation, the first symphony proved a thoroughly acceptable final thesis for examination. It won the unanimous and enthusiastic approval of the Board. But it was more than that: it was a work of undoubted genius, shot through with originality despite its reliance on such models as one would expect a progressive young Leningrader of 1924 to take — Hindemith, Prokofiev, Stravinsky, Scriabin, Tchaikovsky, Mahler. So impressed were the Conservatoire authorities that they decided to arrange for its early performance. Nicolai Malko, conductor of the (now renamed) Leningrad Philharmonic Orchestra, was shown the score and enthusiastically agreed to include it in the final (71st) concert of the 1925–26 season. The cost of copying the parts was met by the Conservatoire, and the performance scheduled to take place on May 12th. At the rehearsal the young composer was jubilant: the orchestra clearly enjoyed the work and everything sounded as he had intended. It was an immediate overwhelming success (one wonders how the other two new and soon forgotten works for chorus and orchestra which had to follow Shostakovich's symphony in the same programme fared!). Conductor and composer were recalled to the platform many times before the remainder of the programme continued. Shostakovich's mother described the scene:

All went more than brilliantly — a splendid orchestra and magnificent execution. The audience listened with enthusiasm and the scherzo had to

Nicolai Malko who conducted the first performance of Shostakovich's first symphony (Reproduced by kind permission of the Malko family)

be played twice. At the end Mitya was called to the stage over and over again. When our handsome young composer appeared, looking almost like a little boy, the enthusiasm turned into one long thunderous ovation. He came to take his bows, sometimes with Malko, sometimes alone.

Malko, who had been 'amazed' by the work ever since hearing it played to him on the piano by the young composer at the Conservatoire, had this to say:

The audience was thrilled, and there was a certain festive mood in the hall. This kind of response is a difficult thing to describe in words, but it is positive in character and, in this instance, there was no mistake about it. Such a feeling usually is apparent when something really outstanding and exceptional is performed. It is not a casual success warmed by casual conditions but a genuine, spontaneous recognition. And so it was on this occasion.

Amidst all the public acclaim, it is interesting to take note of the Shostakovich family's opinion of the work. This is what cousin Tanya, daughter of Sophia's brother Jasha, had to say:

'The criticisms of Mitya's symphony are very good. They say he is exceptionally talented — a genius, remarkable orchestration — but personally I didn't particularly like it. Of course, I am a complete layman in music — although I love it. Mitya played the symphony for us at our house on the piano and of course it sounded all different from the way it came out in the orchestra. In many places one is overwhelmed with a lot of beautiful sounds, but in some places it is very empty — strained. There is a place in the second movement when the orchestra plays a crescendo growing to forte and then suddenly breaks and here the piano comes in with a scale . . . very fast up and down the whole of the keyboard. After the orchestra, the piano sounds like a mosquito. This place struck my nerves; it was as though someone jerked me and woke me up . . .'

This sense of the nervous tension of the music is precisely observed: it is a quality that came to be a hallmark of Shostakovich's style. (And was, of course, a quality of the man also — his chain-smoking and physical nervousness in the presence of people he did not know were legendary.) The composer's aunt Nadejda, living in the USA at the time of the first performance had some interesting things to say about the work when she came to hear it. According to her, much of the material of the symphony was drawn from earlier music — the first movement from a fable in music called *The Dragonfly and the Ant* subsequently published as Op.4; the much admired second movement being an early scherzo

The composer in 1925 at the time of completing his first symphony (Novosti)

from his younger student days; while the expressive bitter-sweet theme of the last movement came from some music which had been written for an unfinished project on Andersen's fairy tale *The Mermaid* at the point where the mermaid swims up through the waters of the lake to the castle where the Prince is holding his festival. On the other hand, since this tune is an upside down version of the funeral march heard on the oboe in the third movement, how can we be sure of Aunt Nadejda's association?

The expressive range of the first symphony is truly remarkable for a boy of nineteen — wit, sarcasm, passionate melody, noble aspiration, contemplation, action, reality, all find their way into a piece whose musical imagery draws from the street, the circus, the theatre, folk music and the great romantic tradition. The light opening of the symphony is deceptive: a tragic dimension is opened up in the later movements. The timpani's menacing interruption half way through the finale is the stroke of Fate, but the masterly way in which the young composer gradually transforms that stroke into a more optimistic mood in the music's progress to the final helter skelter shows an early sense of symphonic breadth and direction.

Certainly the work had to be heard again. Two months later it was given in Moscow, with the composer playing the piano part. The Moscow *Evening Radio* summed up the impression the young musician had made in the following words:

> . . . The absence of the great leaders of our music who have emigrated abroad doesn't frighten us. They have successors.

The first symphony was soon to be heard further afield. The same winter Bruno Walter (who had been Mahler's assistant) was in Leningrad to conduct concerts with the Philharmonic Orchestra and was told — probably by Malko — about the work. It was arranged for Dmitri to play it to him. He was so impressed that he gave an immediate promise to play it in one of his Berlin concerts when he got back. The promise was fulfilled, and the young composer was himself able to attend Walter's performance on 5th May the next year, calling on him to express his thanks late at night. Soviet Russia had discovered its first international star. It was to be the beginning of a burdensome role, but at this stage there was the enjoyment of recognition and the relief of material rewards after many strenuous years.

Chapter 7

The Modernist Years (1927–1936)

Only Beethoven was a forerunner of the revolutionary movement. If you read his letters you will see how often he wrote to his friends that he wished to give new ideas to the public and rouse it to revolt against its masters.

Shostakovich

Amongst the distinguished personages who had been introduced by Malko to Shostakovich's new symphony was an avante garde theatre director, one Vsevolod Emilyevich Meyerhold, whose productions were the talk and scandal of the hour. He had not particularly taken to the work itself, but he was quick to recognise the composer's talent. A telephone call in 1928 from his hotel apartment inviting Dmitri to a meeting led to an invitation to join his theatre company in Moscow as pianist and musical collaborator. There Shostakovich lived in the Meyerhold household in Novinsky Boulevard, and became involved with a personality and milieu whose ideas embodied the spirit of a brilliantly adventurous era, all too soon to be eclipsed by the shadow of Stalin and 'Socialism in one Country'.

There was no shortage of work for the young Soviet composer in what was to prove an eventful decade from both a family and career point of view. He had already met his wife-to-be, Nina Vasilyevna Varzar, grand-daughter of a distinguished economist, and he was shortly to marry — somewhat against the wishes of a possessive and admiring mother — in 1932. As the leading composer/pianist of his generation he was busy with innumerable commissions and first performances. Frequently he found himself overworked and in need of rest and medical treatment, since he suffered from a tubercular condition.

His musical style radically changed, making a break with the impeccable post-romantic craftsmanship of the First Symphony which had already achieved its first American performance in Philadelphia under Stokowski on November 2nd, 1928. Now he aligned himself with the modernist outlook of artists in other

JASS-TWO-STEP
FOX-TROT U
SHIMM
ST. BARBARA A.G.
SANCT BARBARA
LIQUEUR GELB
Die Jazz-Band

A Rodchenko photo-montage, reflecting something of the spirit of the composer's arrangement of *Tea for Two* (1928) while the fox-trot craze raged in Moscow and Leningrad (Museum of Modern Art)

spheres. Like Meyerhold, who becomes something of a guide and mentor during this period, he felt the compulsion to shock and innovate. Like Rodchenko, he rejected the established canons of beauty in art and embraced constructivism with its language of abstraction — its wheels and geometrical patterns. (The Constructivists, however, did not themselves consider such a language 'abstract' — they related it to the materialist outlook of the time, to engineering, mechanics and social utility. In this respect they resembled the Bauhaus group of Germany's Weimar Republic.) Like Mayakovsky, he became active in expressing through his music contempt for old bourgeois values, and threw himself into the social task of re-educating people. A strong note of mockery and fantastic humour was never far absent from his style. He became musical director of the Young Workers' Theatre in Leningrad, he wrote music for films which proclaimed a socialist message and he joined forces with the three artists mentioned above in a production of Mayakovsky's play *The Bedbug* in 1929. Amidst such activity and with such social attitudes it is hardly surprising that one senses some alienation from the family in Marat Street at this time.

Constructivist Poster. Rodchenko's Film Poster (1929) for Eisenstein's *Battleship Potemkin* (SCR)

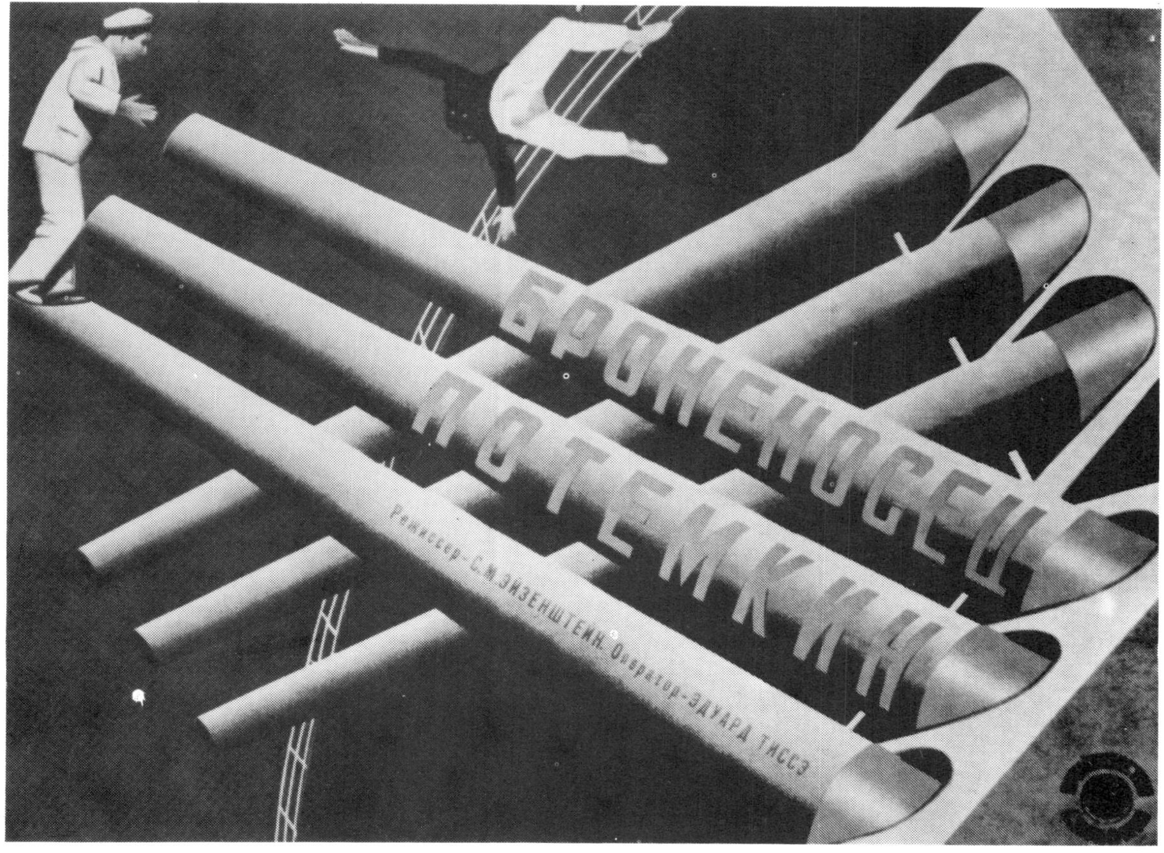

New York Times, December 20th, 1931. Shostakovich interviewed by the American journalist, Rose Lee, in Moscow. (New York Times)

It was a slogan conscious era in which the new genre of poster art was to flourish as a means of getting through to a largely uneducated public — or winning over the bourgeois. And it was to young people in particular that this new message was directed. *The Bedbug* epitomises the aggressive stance of Mayakovsky's group towards Western capitalism; its satire is harsh and uncompromising and its aim was to prick the conscience of all who considered themselves revolutionaries during a time of rapprochement with the bourgeoisie. 'Don't get mad at the bug's antics' ran Mayakovsky's poster for the production. 'they touch NOT YOU but your neighbour'.

As a musician Shostakovich was attracted by the jazz and foxtrotting popular music of the time. The foxtrot was enjoying a vogue in Moscow and Leningrad and one of his most popular pièces d'occasion proved to be a witty, dexterous orchestral

The only surviving page of Shostakovich's music for Mayakovsky's play *The Bedbug*, showing the *Pioneer (Boy Scout) March* for the world of the future. (Reprinted from *Meyerhold: The Art of Conscious Theatre,* by Marjorie L. Hoover (The University of Massachusetts Press, 1974), copyright © 1974 by Marjorie L. Hoover)

DIMITRI SZOSTAKOVITCH

Young Russian Composer Tells of Linking Politics With Creative Work

By ROSE LEE.
Moscow, Dec. 5, 1931.

WHEN the symphony Opus 10, by Dimitri Szostakovitch, was performed in 1928 by the Philadelphia Orchestra and again last Winter by the Philharmonic Orchestra under Toscanini, the critics called it youthful. This was not surprising, for the composition was buoyant in mood and almost naively bold in the liberties it took with the respectable symphonic form. Nobody suspected, however, that it had been composed by a boy of 17. Szostakovitch wrote it in 1924, while he was finishing his course at the Leningrad Conservatory of Music. He has now other works to his credit, soon to be played in America.

In the early days he was still a "Wunderkind," but hated to be reminded of it. Now he has reached the advanced age of 24 and is probably the most successful of the new Russian composers. On the tenth anniversary of the revolution, his Second, or October, symphony was played in four large cities of the Union of Socialist Soviet Republics—Moscow, Leningrad, Kiev and Karkov. Since then it has been heard every year at some October jubilee. His third, or May Day, symphony had its first performance in 1930 and has stirred Russian audiences on each succeeding May Day. It seems as if this pale young man, with the tremulous lips and hands and the manner of a bashful schoolboy, were on the way to becoming a kind of composer-laureate to the Soviet State.

* * *

His earliest American sponsor was Leopold Stokowski, who again visited Leningrad in June of this year and carried away printed copies of the October and May Day symphonies. Presumably one or both of these works will be heard in Philadelphia during future seasons, to show American concertgoers how a rising generation is making music in the cause of socialism. For in Russia there are many youngsters like Szostakovitch, fervent and precocious, who believe themselves elected to point the way to a new era in music. They write a great deal, aspiring always to some perfect form expressive of the new society, as composers of another age aspired to ultimate beauty. In speech they are strangely articulate and quite untroubled by the paradox of the individual artist in a communistic State. They feel as if they had found a key to all questions, if not the immediate mind. Perhaps it is a personal prejudice, but I do not consider Wagner a great composer. It is true he is played rather frequently in Russia today; but we hear him in the same spirit as we go to a museum to study the forms of the old régime. We can learn certain technical lessons from him, but we do not accept him.

"We, as revolutionists, have a different conception of music. Lenin himself said that "music is a means of unifying broad masses of people." Not a leader of masses, perhaps, but certainly an organizing force! For music has the power of stirring specific emotions in those who listen to it. No one can deny that Tchaikovsky's Sixth symphony produces a feeling of despair, while Beethoven's Third awakens one to the joy of struggle. Even the symphonic form, which appears more than any other to be divorced from literary elements, can be said to have a bearing on politics. Thus we regard Scriabine as our bitterest musical enemy.

"Why?" repeated Szostakovitch, staring through his spectacles like an earnest little boy. "Because Scriabine's music tends to an unhealthy eroticism. Also to mysticism and passivity and escape from the realities of life.

"Not that the Soviets are always joyous, or supposed to be. But good music lifts and heartens and lightens people for work and effort. It may be tragic but it must be strong. It is no longer an end in itself, but a vital weapon in the struggle. Because of this, Soviet music will probably develop along different lines from any the world has known. There must be a change! After all, we have entered a new epoch, and history has proved that every age creates its own language. Precisely what form this development in music will take I cannot say, any more than I can say what the idioms of speech will be fifty years from now.

"The notes will be the same!" he concluded with a smile.

* * *

There was something alarming in the assurance of this young man, disposing of the past with no more apparent effort than a twitch of the fingers and a curl of his short upper lip. It was not conceit, however, but the ardor of the acolyte. As far as his own career went, he was quite sincerely modest. He was reluctant to speak of himself at all and had to be prodded with questions. For the past three years, he said, he had really written very little beyond incidental music for films and theatres—

Dimitri Szostakovitch, Russian Composer, Wh
Celebrity by the Distinction and Volum

Wing in politics and the dominance of Stalin's views. Especially it reflects the newly awakened interest in regional culture, a happy by-product of the system of handling national minorities.

For the Russian land is full of untapped musical resources, as the mountains and forests are full of the raw materials of wealth. Mines of melody, the heritage of nearly two hundred racial groups, are becoming accessible fo
ticated com
the concert l
a new flow
upon popula
of folk-then
Szostakovitc
versation, h
hopeful sym
day and pe
way for a
Russia.

arrangement of 'Tea for Two' made as a bet with the conductor Nicolai Malko that he could complete the task in 45 minutes. The arrangement was incorporated into the ballet *The Golden Age*, another satire on Western capitalism. Soon, however, he found that the piece (through being played separately under the baton of Malko) was likely to get him into trouble with the moral

An avant garde trio. Shostakovich, Meyerhold and Mayakovsky (standing) during work on 'The bedbug', 1929 (Novosti)

The avant garde, realist young composer. A page from the second symphony ('Symphonic Dedication to October, — 1927) which describes a brutal street killing in the 1917 Revolution, witnessed by Shostakovich as a boy. (Reprinted by permission of Anglo-Soviet Music Press Ltd)

custodians of Soviet virtue. The 'foxtrotting West' had become in the eyes of officialdom a symbol of bourgeois decadence and 'the light genre' was condemned by Anatole Lunacharsky, the People's Commissar of Education at a party conference on music in these words:

> The bourgeoisie would like man to live not so much by his head as by his sexual organs . . . The fundamental element of the fox trot derives from

mechanisation, suppressed eroticism and a desire to deaden feeling through drugs . . .

In order to cover himself Shostakovich wrote a letter to 'The Proletarian Musician' (a Journal dedicated to the propagation of aggressively anti-bourgeois views) in which he suggested ways of combatting 'the light genre'. In the post-script he added

> I consider it a political mistake on my part to have granted Conductor Malko permission to arrange my orchestration of 'Tahiti Trot' since 'Tahiti Trot', when performed without an appropriate setting might create the impression that I am an advocate of the light genre. A proper injunction was sent by me to Conductor Malko about three months ago.

During these years the young composer proved himself adept in all genres — symphonic, theatre, ballet, film, solo piano and chamber music. One of his first ventures after leaving the Conservatoire had been the ultra modernistic *Aphorisms* for solo piano — ten short pieces which deliberately flew in the face of traditionalism, to the sorrow and dismay of his former teachers at the Conservatoire. The same year, 1927, he composed his Symphony No. 2, subtitled 'Symphonic Dedication to October' in response to a commission for an appropriate work for the tenth anniversary of the Revolution. This piece, for chorus and orchestra, is an early example of Shostakovich's programme music on the theme of the Russian Revolution of 1917 and its heralding of a new dawn for the proletariat. It shows the influence of constructivist 'abstract' art in its machine-inspired textures, Soviet realism (as well as describing a brutal murder he had witnessed as a young boy in 1917 there is a factory hooter signal preparing for the final section and a passage of choral speech over a side drum roll) and 'poster consciousness' in its collective appeal to the original spirit of protest and idealism behind Lenin's revolution. (The symphony was praised at its first performance, with some reservations, but soon fell into neglect, only to be revived in the avant garde West of the late 1960's.)

But perhaps the most outrageous work of these years was his first opera, *The Nose*, which was produced at the Malyi Theatre, Leningrad, on 18th January 1930. In an article written at the time of this production, entitled 'Why the Nose?', Shostakovich explained that he had turned to Gogol because he found his colleagues in literature either unwilling or unable to collaborate with him in the provision of a libretto. He chose *The Nose* because it was a satire on the epoch of Nicholas I and seemed stronger than any other story by Gogol, finding the language more sparkling and more expressive than in any other of this author's *Petersburg Tales*. In the opera, Gogol's serious, matter-of-fact realism in narrating this strange, comic tale about a self-opinionated civil servant whose nose left him to assume a higher rank, was counterpointed by his own non-satirical music which, though descriptive, did not 'wisecrack'. One of the most grotesque scenes in the opera was inspired by this passage from Gogol's text:

> Collegiate Assessor Kovalev . . . awoke early that morning. And when he had done so he made the 'B-r-rh!' with his lips which he always did when he had been asleep — he himself could not have said why. Then he stretched himself, had handed to him a small mirror from the table nearby, and set himself to inspect a pimple which had broken out on his nose the night before. But, to his unbounded astonishment, there was only a flat patch on his face where the nose should have been!

Shostakovich with his wife Nina in 1932, the year of their marriage, with their close friend Ivan Sollertinsky (Novosti)

The music of *The Nose* was much influenced by a great new opera from Germany which had taken Leningrad by storm in June 1927, conducted by Vladimir Dranischnikov and described by the

composer in a telegram to his wife as a 'tumultuous success'. This was Alban Berg's *Wozzeck* — a tale about a common soldier driven to murder and delusions by an uncomprehending world of manipulative characters who use him as a means for furthering their own ambitions and greed. The ideological appeal to the Soviet outlook of such a story is obvious. But Shostakovich no less eagerly devoured the musical style of the opera and copied many of Berg's musical-dramatic devices in *The Nose*. As in his other works written since the first symphony, the composer showed that he could be uncompromising in his pursuit of innovation, and he had powerful, articulate support from a newfound and close friend of these years, Ivan Ivanovich Sollertinsky — one of the most brilliant scholar-musicians to have emerged since the revolution. Wrote Sollertinsky in his urgent, prophetic style:

> . . . he (Shostakovich) is perhaps the first among Russian opera composers to make his heroes speak not in conventional arias and cantilenas but in living language, setting everyday speech to music . . . The opera theatre is at the crossroads. The birth of Soviet Opera is not far off . . .

Amongst Shostakovich's many friends and admirers, Ivan Sollertinsky was perhaps the closest and most influential. The possessor of a deep historical awareness of all music, both European and Russian, keenly aware of Mahler's importance to Soviet composers in the development of the symphony (he wrote a study of this composer in 1932) and naturally attracted to what was new and interesting in art, Sollertinsky had a mind teeming with ideas. Despite the profundity and breadth of his outlook he had a ready wit, and was quickly recognised as a brilliant lecturer who was able to draw from all that was best in European art and thought in moulding the new Soviet consciousness. Such brilliance was not to escape censure in Stalin's purges of Soviet Russia's intellectual life, but until his death in 1944 Sollertinsky was able to keep his position as one of the most stimulating products of a new school of philosopher-sociologist musicians headed by the towering figure of Boris Asafiev.

There is every indication that, but for Stalin's coming to power, the young Shostakovich would have pursued his brilliant career as a theatre composer. The initial success of his next opera, *Lady Macbeth of the Mtensk District* was leading him on to plan an operatic cycle of Wagnerian dimensions, with a socially 'realistic' theme that was to extol the role of Russian womanhood. In an interview during the successful run of *Lady Macbeth* he said:

> I want to write a Soviet 'Ring of the Nibelung'. This will be the first operatic tetralogy about women, of which Lady Macbeth will be the

Rheingold. This will be followed by an opera written around the heroine of the People's Will Movement (Sofia Perofskaya, who organised the assassination of Alexander II, and who was hanged with the rest of the 'First-of-March Men'). Then a woman of our century; and finally I will create our Soviet heroine, who will combine in her character the qualities of the woman of today and tomorrow — from Larissa Reisner to the Dnieprostroy working-woman, Jennie Romanko. This theme is the leit-motiv of my daily thought and will be for the next ten years.

Lady Macbeth was first performed on the 22nd January 1934, at the Malyi Theatre, Leningrad, and ran triumphantly for two years reaching audiences in New York before being officially torpedoed after a visit to the Opera by Stalin in January 1936. In March it reached London. Benjamin Britten wrote in his diary after attending the first performance on 18th March:

Of course it is idle to pretend that this is great music throughout — it is stage music and as such must be considered. There is some terrific music in the entr'acts. But I will defend it through thick & thin against these charges of 'lack of style'. People will not differentiate between style & manner. It is the composer's heritage to take what he wants from whom he wants — & to write music. There is a consistency of style & method throughout. The satire is biting & brilliant. It is never boring for a second . . .

The first Shostakovich was to hear of official Soviet disapproval of his opera was when he opened his copy of *Pravda* on the morning of 28th January 1936, on a trip to Arkhangelsk with Viktor Kubatsky, the cellist, with whom he was giving performances of his new cello sonata. There, in the left had corner on page 3, was a three column denunciation of the opera, entitled 'Chaos instead of Music'.

From the first moment, the listener is shocked by a deliberately dissonant, confused stream of sound' ran the review. 'Fragments of melody, embryonic phrases appear — only to disappear again in the din, the grinding, and the screaming . . . This music is built on the basis of rejecting opera . . . which carries into the theatre and the music the most negative gestures of "Meyerholdism" infinitely multiplied. Here we have "leftist" confusion instead of natural, human music . . .

It was rumoured that the author of this denunciation was one Andrei Zhdanov, the new leader of the Communist Party in Leningrad and Stalin's spokesman on Cultural Policy in the Central Committee. (In 1934 Zhdanov had presided over the convention of the Union of Soviet Writers which first introduced the concept of 'Socialist Realism'.)

СУМБУР ВМЕСТО МУЗЫКИ

Об опере «Леди Макбет Мценского уезда»

Вместе с общим культурным ростом в нашей стране выросла и потребность в хорошей музыке. Никогда и нигде композиторы не имели перед собой такой благодарной аудитории. Народные массы ждут хороших песен, но также и хороших инструментальных произведений, хороших опер.

Некоторые театры как новинку, как достижение преподносят новой, выросшей культурно советской публике оперу Шостаковича «Леди Макбет Мценского уезда». Услужливая музыкальная критика превозносит до небес оперу, создает ей громкую славу. Молодой композитор вместо деловой и серьезной критики, которая могла бы помочь ему в дальнейшей работе, выслушивает только восторженные комплименты.

Слушателя с первой же минуты ошарашивает в опере нарочито нестройный, сумбурный поток звуков. Обрывки мелодии, зачатки музыкальной фразы тонут, вырываются, снова исчезают в грохоте, скрежете и визге. Следить за этой «музыкой» трудно, запомнить ее невозможно.

Так в течение почти всей оперы. На сцене пение заменено криком. Если композитору случается попасть на дорожку простой и понятной мелодии, то он немедленно, словно испугавшись такой беды, бросается в дебри музыкального сумбура, местами превращающегося в какофонию. Выразительность, которой требует слушатель, заменена бешеным ритмом. Музыкальный шум должен выразить страсть.

Это все не от бездарности композитора, не от его неумения в музыке выразить простые и сильные чувства. Это музыка, умышленно сделанная «шиворот навыворот», — так, чтобы ничего не напоминало классическую оперную музыку, ничего не было общего с симфоническими звучаниями, с простой, общедоступной музыкальной речью. Это музыка, которая построена по тому же принципу отрицания оперы, по какому левацкое искусство вообще отрицает в театре простоту, реализм, понятность образа, естественное звучание слова. Это — перенесение в оперу, в музыку наиболее отрицательных черт «мейерхольдовщины» в умноженном виде. Это левацкий сумбур вместо естественной, человеческой музыки. Способность хорошей музыки захватывать массы приносится в жертву мелкобуржуазным формалистическим потугам, претензиям создать оригинальность приемами дешевого оригинальничанья. Это игра в заумные вещи, которая может кончиться очень плохо.

Опасность такого направления в советской музыке ясна. Левацкое уродство в опере растет из того же источника, что и левацкое уродство в живописи, в поэзии, в педагогике, в науке. Мелкобуржуазное «новаторство» ведет к отрыву от подлинного искусства, от подлинной науки, от подлинной литературы.

Автору «Леди Макбет Мценского уезда» пришлось заимствовать у джаза его нервозную, судорожную, припадочную музыку, чтобы придать «страсть» своим героям.

В то время как наша критика — в том числе и музыкальная — клянется именем социалистического реализма, сцена преподносит нам в творении Шостаковича грубейший натурализм. Однотонно, в зверином обличии представлены все — и купцы и народ. Хищница-купчиха, дорвавшаяся путем убийств к богатству и власти, представлена в виде какой-то «жертвы» буржуазного общества. Бытовой повести Лескова навязан смысл, какого в ней нет.

И все это грубо, примитивно, вульгарно. Музыка крякает, ухает, пыхтит, задыхается, чтобы как можно натуральнее изобразить любовные сцены. И «любовь» размазана во всей опере в самой вульгарной форме. Купеческая двуспальная кровать занимает центральное место в оформлении. На ней разрешаются все «проблемы». В таком же грубо-натуралистическом стиле показана смерть от отравления, сечение почти на самой сцене.

Композитор, видимо, не поставил перед собой задачи прислушаться к тому, чего ждет, чего ищет в музыке советская аудитория. Он словно нарочно зашифровал свою музыку, перепутал все звучания в ней так, чтобы дошла его музыка только до потерявших здоровый вкус эстетов-формалистов. Он прошел мимо требований советской культуры изгнать грубость и дикость из всех углов советского быта. Это воспевание купеческой похотливости некоторые критики называют сатирой. Ни о какой сатире здесь и речи не может быть. Всеми средствами и музыкальной и драматической выразительности автор старается привлечь симпатии публики к грубым и вульгарным стремлениям и поступкам купчихи Катерины Измайловой.

«Леди Макбет» имеет успех у буржуазной публики за границей. Не потому ли похваливает ее буржуазная публика, что опера эта сумбурна и абсолютно аполитична? Не потому ли, что она щекочет извращенные вкусы буржуазной аудитории своей дергающейся, крикливой, неврастенической музыкой?

Наши театры приложили немало труда, чтобы тщательно поставить оперу Шостаковича. Актеры обнаружили значительный талант в преодолении шума, крика и скрежета оркестра. Драматической игрой они старались возместить мелодийное убожество оперы. К сожалению, от этого еще ярче выступили ее грубо-натуралистические черты. Талантливая игра заслуживает признательности, затраченные усилия — сожаления.

Pravda, 28th January, 1936. The article 'Chaos instead of Music' denouncing Shostakovich's opera *Lady Macbeth of the Mtensk District*. (Pravda)

As a matter of musical fact, *Lady Macbeth* was an opera in the grand nineteenth century traditions, Verdian in its range of characterisation and humanity and much less of an avant garde venture than *The Nose* or the second symphony had been. But Stalin was concerned about its content — its Straussian realism in the portrayal of certain bedroom scenes, the unpleasant violence and tragic power of its subject matter ('happy endings' were important as propaganda) and, perhaps above all he feared the sheer compelling genius behind its musico-dramatic conception. The opera had been well received initially, it lent itself readily to a Soviet view of progress in denouncing the corruption of Tsarist nineteenth century merchant life, it was splendidly Russian in its treatment of character and situation, but it encouraged audiences to think rather too much for themselves, to draw fine moral distinctions which were inappropriate in the context of the official 'new and beautiful' life implicit in the formula of 'Socialist Realism' — the new cultural orthodoxy. Stalin required conformity above all in the achievement of his programme of 'Socialism in one Country' (which meant the abandonment of Lenin's and Trotsky's goal of a 'Communist International'); creative intellectuals like Meyerhold and Shostakovich posed a threat to him, as did Schoenberg, Brecht and Weill to Hitler in Nazi Germany.

Before the thunderbolt fell Shostakovich had been working on a new symphony — his fourth, which had, in all probability, been intended as a personal response to a new-found enthusiasm amongst composers and intellectuals for the idea of Soviet Symphonism. At this stage Shostakovich had not abandoned his position as a musical innovator. At a conference on Soviet Symphonism in February 1935 Shostakovich had said:

> We Soviet composers do not know enough about Western compositions . . . We should have a seminar at the Composers' Union to become acquainted with the musical culture of the West; there is much that is interesting and instructive.

Earlier, in 1932, Sollertinsky had urged Soviet composers to follow the example of Mahler. 'Mahler is closer to us than Debussy or Stravinsky, Richard Strauss or Hindemith,' he had written, citing amongst other things, his 'attempt to reach a human collective' and the absence in his music of sensationalism used for its own sake.

The fourth symphony was Shostakovich's most Mahlerian work and was both an end and a beginning in the composer's development. It was an end of his involvement with the Western avant garde and expressionism — the culture on which Stalin was to impose his embargo; it was a beginning of a new kind of symphony that was to achieve sober maturity and official recognition in his fifth. But in view of the *Lady Macbeth* attack and Shostakovich's subsequent disgrace amongst his colleagues (his works began to disappear rapidly from theatre and concert hall at this time) he decided to withdraw the symphony on the eve of its scheduled first performance under Fritz Stiedry. To have performed such a wild and fundamentally pessimistic work in such a hostile climate would have been unwise. The withdrawal of the fourth symphony came to be interpreted as a gesture of reappraisal in the light of public criticism. As for the symphony itself, Shostakovich did not destroy it. He kept it in his drawer like a secret diary, locked away until such a time that would permit its contents to be disclosed. It had to wait twenty-five years.

Chapter 8

Public and Private Artist (1934–1938)

. . . the grandiose vistas of the tragically tense Fifth Symphony with its philosophical search.

Pravda

The fifth symphony, composed when Stalin's 'Yezhovshchina'* was in full spate, raises so many important issues in reviewing Shostakovich's career that it must mark a reflective pause in our narrative. One is tempted to say, indeed, that the fifth symphony of 1937 was a watershed in his career — like Beethoven's *Eroica* of 1803 — and inaugurated a second 'period' of compositional development. That the composer himself regarded the work as a landmark in his creative life is shown in his backward references to its themes and gestures in several subsequent works.

Interestingly enough, both his first and last string quartets make reference to the fifth symphony, and further unmistakable allusions crop up in many other places. The fifth symphony is the first composition of Shostakovich to attach semantic value to a rhythmic motto which, like the later DSCH motto, became a fingerprint of his style. The two shorts and a long (or anapaest) on a repeated note is here a motif of aspiration or striving which features in every movement (in the second movement, however, it is parodied), and here again a parallel with Beethoven is unavoidable. Beethoven's fifth symphony makes use of a similar rhythmic device ('thus Fate knocks at the door') in all four of its movements — and it is not unreasonable to suppose that Shostakovich was conscious of the need to unify his work in some grand, elemental way which would link up with his great revolutionary predecessor. The programme of the two symphonies, indeed, is almost identical. Each is a 'striving' work in four movements whose finale resolves the doubts and tragic struggle of the preceding parts. The parallel with Beethoven is even more striking when we remember that Beethoven also adopted the rhythmic motto of his fifth symphony in subsequent works such as the fourth piano concerto and the 'Appassionata'

The composer with a portrait of Beethoven behind him. Shostakovich had a strong sense of identification — social, historical and creative — with the great European symphonist. (A photograph taken in Leningrad, 1941, when the composer was at work on his seventh symphony (Novosti)

*Literally 'Yezhov Rule'.

Sonata. It must be emphasised that for Shostakovich, the example of Beethoven was supreme. In 1941 his friend Sollertinsky was to write.

> In our musical world there still remain traces of various Beethovenian concepts about the development of the symphony. The reason for this is that in the history of musical-culture there exists only one culminating point in the development of the symphony. This culminating point is marked by Beethoven, by his expression of the 'heroic' in his fifth or ninth symphonies. . . . Every composer has the right to alter the form of the symphony so long as he remains basically true and faithful to the Beethovenian method of symphonic construction. . . . The very terms 'Beethovenianist' and 'symphonist' are not really separable.

In presenting the idea of struggle and catastrophe in his fifth symphony Shostakovich was well aware that some advocates of Soviet Realism would question the 'correctness' of his musical ideology. As Stalin's policy of 'Socialism in one Country' hardened into a bureaucratic system of repression and terror there was a clear line of orthodoxy from which artists and thinkers deviated at their peril. Composers were now expected to submit their work to collective discussion by their colleagues. 'Pessimism' was considered 'bourgeois degeneracy' and happy endings were essential to the image of a new, aspiring society. 'Among the services rendered by the victorious proletariat of the Soviet Union' wrote Maxim Gorki in 1934 'one must include the fact that its amazing and heroical labours have purged the world of the rust and mould of pessimism'. In defending his symphony from the anticipated attacks of people and organisations inside Russia who were all too ready to sound the 'bourgeois decadence' alarm Shostakovich felt obliged to write as follows:

> We often doubt whether a tragic style is at all permissible in Soviet Art. But that, I believe, is only because tragedy can easily mean Fate or Pessimism. Personally, I think that Soviet Tragedy, as a type, has a right to exist; but Soviet Tragedy should be permeated with a 'positive' idea — like Shakespeare's ever-living pathos.

The simplified style of the fifth symphony had much about it that chimed with the new cultural orthodoxy — Shostakovich had during its period of gestation worked to acquire a style of address which, in blending the rhetoric of Tchaikovsky and Mahler, would guarantee public comprehensibility, that 'grand, new simplicity' for which Prokofiev, on his return to Russia, had called in 1934. (At this time the composer found a conductor who from now on would champion his symphonic works with total commitment. Such a find is always a vital link in the relationship

Yevgeny Mravinsky — a close colleague and life-long conductor of Shostakovich's music, whose association with the composer began with the fifth symphony. A photograph taken in his later years. (See also Chapter 10) (SCR)

between a composer and his public. Yevgeny Alexandrovich Mravinsky was thirty-four when he took charge of the first performance of the fifth symphony in Leningrad. He became musical director of the Leningrad Philharmonic Orchestra the following year and still holds this post. The sixth, eighth, ninth and tenth symphonies were all given their first performances under Mravinsky's direction, and Shostakovich was to dedicate one of his greatest and, from a Soviet point of view, most controversial works — the eighth symphony — to him.)

But how genuine is the happy ending of the fifth symphony? Shostakovich is reported as having this to say to his young friend, Solomon Volkov, towards the end of his life:

> I think that it is clear to everyone what happens in the Fifth. The rejoicing is forced, created under a threat, as in Boris Godunov. It's as if someone were beating you with a stick and saying, 'your business is rejoicing, your business is rejoicing, and you rise, shakily and go marching off muttering 'Our business is rejoicing, our business is rejoicing . . .' Fadeyev heard it, and he wrote in his diary, for his personal use, that the finale of the Fifth is irreparable tragedy . . .

Whatever doubt exists as to the ultimate message of the fifth symphony there can be no question as to the tragic end and, indeed, personally despairing import of the fourth.

The fifth symphony cannot be seen in isolation from the fourth, which, as we have already stated, Shostakovich withdrew before its scheduled première in 1936. There was a time (before the fourth was well known) when the fifth was seen as its very antithesis, but, in fact, the two symphonies have much in common and even share common themes. The first movement of the fourth established a type of first movement which the composer used again and again through to the tenth. This is a large-scale, moderately paced movement in which themes are contrasted, developed and 'brutalised' to a climax of destructive fury and brought back in reverse order with their original identities transformed. In this all-important recapitulation section the transformations can be very startling. Thus in the first movement of the fourth symphony what was originally quiet and intimate becomes tragically tense and martial in tone, what was originally grandly tragic becomes subdued and grotesque, the 'public' becomes 'private', the 'collective' becomes the 'individual' and vice versa. Such a sense of contrast and the identity of opposites gives to Shostakovich's music a dialectical quality of 'becoming', of thesis, antithesis and synthesis which can be partially explained in terms of the historical philosophy of Hegel and Marx who saw history as a continuous spiral of development. The relationship between theory and practice is a question that has much possessed Russian artists and intellectuals: Tchaikovsky worried about his capacity to mould his ideas in accordance with theories of form; Tolstoy observed life in all its variety and yet sought to impose a reductive ethical simplicity on such experience; Meyerhold sought the psychological truth behind appearance in his application of symbolist and constructivist theory to acting; the Constructivists themselves eschewed photographic 'reality' in favour of a way of seeing that readily lent itself to Marxian doctrine ('It is not the consciousness of men that determines their being, but, on the contrary, their social being that determines their consciousness'). Similarly, Shostakovich in his music sought to forge a technique that was to some extent shaped by the philosophical and ideological principles uderlying new social aspirations. The fourth symphony essays a wide, truly non élitist canvas of musical characterisation and genre in its attempt to express a new consciousness. In all this, the musical example of Mahler may have been an example, but the socio-aesthetic theories of such inspired thinkers as Asafiev and Sollertinsky were no less influential. 'The essence of the Soviet Symphony must be: universal scope, many varied themes, types, genres, intonations and expressive means' Sollertinsky had written. 'Musicians from all over the world shall listen to its voice, as shall all the listeners and everyone who is looking for an escape from the torments of their own society and looking for a new road to follow.' And in digesting the ideas of these men Shostakovich gave birth to a new type of symphony in the fourth which neither his brilliantly conservative first nor his avant garde second prefigured; a vast sprawling canvas which, like Tolstoy's *War and Peace,* could embrace the public and the private, the epic and the personal, the various in conflict with a sense of unifying wholeness. Few pages in the history of music can compare with the universal sense of gloom and despair in the Coda of this work where Shostakovich brings back his grotesquely subdued funeral march originally intoned by the solo bassoon in a cataclysmic transformation for the whole orchestra, a 'burn up' besides which even Bruckner may seem to pale. Since Shostakovich was completing this symphony at the very time his public career seemed in ruins after the attack on *Lady Macbeth* it is not unreasonable to suppose that we have here an expression (universalised, of course, as all such experiences must be) of the composer's own sense of despair. As Robert Layton has written,' the closing section of this score leaves no doubt (in my mind anyway) that this symphony records a tragic spiritual experience'.

Another writer has spoken of 'the passionately personal and intimate symphonist we encounter in such works as the Fourth symphony'. Referring to its 'ferociously autobiographical' style the same author goes on to say

> But the truth is that Shostakovich always seems to have exploited two veins in his symphonic art, the explicitly public and the explicitly private, and has had at his disposal a powerful, versatile style which accommodates both worlds.

The violence and destructive power that is unleashed in the fourth symphony pulled urgently against formal coherence and reasonable proportions. Shostakovich, in one of his frequent bouts of public self-criticism, while admitting that there were parts he liked, said that it suffered from 'grandiosomania'. And yet, as we have already seen, the first movement established a basic pattern of form and content that served in the subsequent so-called 'war' symphonies. We must, therefore, be on our guard against seeing the fifth as a total rejection of the fourth. Certainly the trends towards emotional excess and unwieldy proportions are now held in check, but the fourth struck out on a path that Shostakovich continued to follow: from now on the symphony was to be a comprehensive, large scale canvas on an appropriately heroic theme. The momentum of such a work could be explained in terms of Hegel's dialectic: thesis, antithesis, synthesis.

As a release from the pressures of symphonic oratory Shostakovich turned to the private medium of the string quartet, and with his first quartet opened up a new chapter in his musical autobiography. The string quartet could perhaps, if need be, provide a confessional outlet for an embattled public figure, and as his career developed Shostakovich came to use the medium almost, as Gerald Abraham has suggested, like a secret diary rich in cryptograms and subtle allusions. In this private dialogue for four musicians the composer could treat his audience as eaves-droppers on an intimate conversation rather than as a national gathering to be served with moral precepts and grandiose rhetoric.

The first quartet was a light, unpretentious affair composed during May and June 1938, and performed on 10th October at Leningrad by the Glazunov Quartet. Shostakovich began to write it 'without any particular thoughts or feelings' during a fallow period after the fifth symphony 'thinking that nothing would come of it'. 'But then,' he goes on to say 'work on the quartet attracted me very much and I wrote it extraordinarily quickly. You mustn't look for any particular depths in this, my first quartet opus . . . I would call it a "Spring" Quartet'.

Here is the private artist at work. The piece is short, innocent, very classical in its style and structure: in fact the complete reverse of the fifth symphony. (One could, perhaps, compare the public and private styles of the fifth symphony and first quartet with that of one of Leningrad's great architects of the nineteenth century — Rastrelli. The heroic scale of his Winter Palace is the symphony to the string quartet of the Summer Palace of Peter the Great.) True, there are half memories of the symphony — in a little fragment of violin tune that emerges quite soon, or in the shape of the scherzo tune, with its hint of Mahler's 'St Anthony and the Fishes' (on which song he had previously modelled the scherzo of his fifth symphony) — but that heroic world is far distant, and perhaps in writing this first quartet the composer was reminded of his first encounter with the medium as a child listening to his neighbour's musical evenings in Podolskaya Street. The music may be simple but the technique is masterly and utterly idiosyncratic: the work shows that the composer was equally self assured when he felt the urge to be laconic and confidential. At the same time there is a sense of continuity from movement to movement, for Shostakovich's contrasts are always rooted in his technique of transforming an idea into its opposite. The quartet, in other words, is not just a suite of four movements: it is an organic whole. Before writing his next quartet, however, there was to be a whole series of massively public works. Not until he had completed his sixth, seventh and eighth symphonies was there to be a return to the medium, by which time the composer was beginning to view chamber music in a different, more soul-searching light. Stalin and the War Years were to lead to a deepening of the composer's sense of human suffering, of tragedy and irony, and with it a sharper awareness of the conflict between official expectations and the voice of artistic conscience.

Chapter 9

World War 2 and Russia's 'Great Patriotic War' (1939–1945)

How many rusty beds and bunks
littered the street those days!
They hunched down among the ruins
senselessly trying to screen them.
Their sombre, bony dance twirled
everywhere the ground was being dug for vegetables . . .
And for no particular reason they gathered
here and there on the embankment — dark and bare
as though Dystrophia, the enemy,
wanted a place to rest up nights.

Olga Berggolts

In Europe Armageddon loomed. In Italy Fascism — in the person of Mussolini — took control of a chaotic domestic situation. In Germany National Socialism (or Nazism) found in Hitler an even greater evil than Italy's Mussolini. Hitler was on the march — into Austria and the Rhineland. The Spanish Civil War of 1936–1939 involved a young generation of idealists, intellectuals and adventurers — the International Brigade — who

Picasso's Guernica 'I should . . . like to compare the music of Shostakovich with the later works of Pablo Picasso. This refers to such canvasses as 'The Destruction of Guernica', in which the artist pilloried the fascist murderers'. Martynov (© S.P.A.D.E.M. Paris, 1981)

were concerned about what was at stake: the destruction by Franco and his fascist-aided forces of a legitimate native government. Soviet Russia (whose bright new image was by now getting tarnished as Stalin's reputation as a latter-day Ivan the Terrible grew) had its international credit somewhat restored through coming to the aid of the Republican side, but in so doing divided the loyalists as they pondered the implications of such aid. At the Basque town of Guernica the German air force massacred an innocent population — a crime against humanity which Picasso has symbolised for ever in his painting of that name. Appeasement of Hitler's jackboot policies became personified in the pathetic figure of the British Prime Minister, Neville Chamberlain who, after a quadruple conference of France, Britain, Italy and Germany at Munich returned with a piece of paper signed by himself and Hitler saying 'I believe this is peace for our time'. The invasion of Czechoslovakia by Hitler and Albania by Mussolini hardly confirmed his belief. What followed is admirably summed up by H. G. Wells in his *Short History of the World:*

> The British Government now at last realised what was on the way. (The French was paralysed; the other European states were helpless; the United States was still living in its fool's paradise.) There was only one serious ally available: Russia, which was Hitler's special abomination and against whom his savagest rhetoric had always been used. Reluctantly Britain sent a mission to Moscow, headed by a minor official, to negotiate a last-minute treaty. But now it was too late. Stalin had long ago jettisoned the principles of the Russian revolution, and saw no profound objection to a treaty with the Nazis. He regarded the Nazis and the West as two suitors for his favours; Hitler, who for all his manias was far the cleverer politician, was delighted to offer him better terms. Hitler's calculation was simple. Germany, between France and Russia, with Britain holding the seas, would have been a nut in a nutcracker. Once Russia was removed, war would be safe for Germany. Russia could be dealt with later. But Stalin had as little geographical knowledge as he had political principles; to the stupor of the world, and even of many Communists, Communist Russia signed a pact with Nazi Germany. What its terms in detail were was not known, and may never be fully known, but it was soon shown to include a new partition of Poland. On the first day of September, 1939, knowing that the alliance signed with France and Britain meant the beginning of a new world war, Hitler invaded Poland.

Hitler did not attack Russia until June 1941. Meanwhile Stalin was able to settle an old score. On 20th August 1940 Leon Trotsky was assassinated in exile in Mexico at the dictate of Stalin; on his desk was his unfinished biography of Stalin, whom he had called in 1926 'gravedigger of the revolution'. In Russia itself the purges had begun to subside as Stalin's foreign policy concerned itself with a cruel war against Finland (from which Russia emerged with its borders enlarged) and expansion into Rumania — a move which, together with further subsequent conflicts of interest in the Balkans, did not please Hitler. When the war with Germany finally did come it is said to have surprised the people of Russia rather more than it did the politicians, who had seen it as inevitable for some time.

There had been no shortage of serious and tragic statements in music in the years leading up to 1939 and the Second World War. We are accustomed to thinking of art as prophetic: the artist can see further ahead than the politician. As far back as 1924 the last pages of Sibelius' seventh symphony had expressed a grim and resigned stoicism; Berg's *Wozzeck* (planned as a symphonic whole) inhabited a nightmare world of persecution and madness, for all its compassionate humanity; the same year as Shostakovich began work on his cataclysmic fourth symphony in 1934 Berg (shortly before his death) completed his dark Violin Concerto as a Requiem 'in memory of an angel'; in England, Walton wrote his angry, protesting first symphony (and got stuck — as well he may! — for a finale) and Vaughan Williams completed his violent fourth. Bartok, too, produced works of a dark intensity during the middle to late thirties — the *Music for Strings, Percussion and Celeste* and, in 1939, the sixth quartet with its desolate finale. In Hitler's Nazi Germany both Hindemith and Schoenberg had been forced to leave the country — and from Schoenberg in American emigration there came music which contains more than a hint of crisis and dark foreboding — the sombre opening of the Violin Concerto, the dance round the Golden Calf of *Moses and Aaron*, the fateful return of E flat minor in the second Chamber Symphony are passages which spring to mind.

As for Shostakovich in his lonely and dangerous eminence as Soviet Russia's biggest musical talent, there is no knowing how far his private sensibility was touched by what was going on in Europe or what he thought of Stalin's alignment with the Nazi menace. But like every Russian intellectual at that time, he had lost friends and colleagues in the Stalin purge — foremost amongst them his stimulating patron of the late twenties, Meyerhold, arrested in 1939 and dying in custody the following year.

Since the completion of the fifth symphony and first quartet Shostakovich had been living in Leningrad with his wife and two young children, Galya (born in 1936) and Maxim (born in 1938) in a spacious apartment provided by the Composers' Union at the House of Composers. He had, in 1937, been appointed a professor at the Leningrad Conservatoire — a job that entailed considerable administrative duties as well as teaching. (He was concerened, for instance, with the chairmanship of both composition and piano examining boards in the summer of 1941.) Since completing his first quartet he had been productive as a writer of film scores for the Soviet film unit *Lenfilm*. Stalin himself attached great value to Shostakovich the film composer; as Volkov puts it, Shostakovich was able, in his film scores, 'to render unto Caesar the things that were Caesar's'.

We have an intimate portrait of Shostakovich at this time from his friend and biographer, D. Rabinovich:

He was not very tall, although taller than he seemed at first glance, slim, with a fine-cut face and nervous hands that were never quite still and a permanently unruly forelock — despite his thirty odd years he gave one the impression of youthfulness. Even as long ago as that, an interesting contrast was noticeable in him: his kindly eyes flashed at times with merriment, at others with mischief, and in the same face, thin, tightly-pressed lips were a sign of will-power, of stubbornness even.

His character is a strange mixture of opposites. By his own admission he adores life. He does not like to be alone and when in company may be the focal point of a conversation. But for all that he has constant thoughts of his own that he keeps to himself. His nervous fingers are often playing a melody that he alone can hear. I have frequently observed him: he is talking excitedly to his friends, telling them something about yesterday's concert, or, with still greater fervour, he is describing a recent football match, gesticulating excitedly and jumping up at times from his seat. . . . And if you look into the eyes behind his big, horn-rimmed glasses you get the idea that actually only one little corner of his mind is present in the room, the rest of him is far, far away.

He had begun to plan another symphony in 1939. Conscious of his national role, he announced that it was to be a 'Lenin' symphony in which Mayakovsky's poem on Lenin was to receive a choral and orchestral setting. 'The Symphony', wrote Shostakovich, 'will make use of the words as well as the melodies of popular songs about Lenin'. Such a grandiose theme aroused much speculation and anticipation, but the plan was not to be realised. Instead Shostakovich produced a work which, like its predecessor, the fifth, was purely instrumental though utterly different in conception. For although the serious, pondering first movement of the sixth symphony begins with a heroic theme, opening up grand vistas in the manner of Mahler, yet its continuation in a grotesque scherzo and irresponsibly gay finale seemed to its first audiences both inconsequential and improper. Like all great symphonists, Shostakovich found it impossible to repeat himself from one work to the next. He believed in keeping his public guessing. The work was stoutly defended by Sollertinsky, who found in it a profound inner unity based on the principle of lyrical modulation from 'direct' (=straight) to 'indirect' (=grotesque). Indeed, this symphony has a splendid momentum, and the finale is perhaps Shostakovich's most purely exhilarating in its progress from elegant wit to sheer circus high spirits. We may note in this symphony too how consistent Shostakovich's style and inspiration were to prove over the years: the slow, unfolding 'ground swell' of the first movement is father to the same mood in the historic tenth, conceived some fourteen years later. Shortly after this symphony, on 23rd November 1940 at Moscow, came the first performance of the Piano Quintet which won the composer a Stalin prize of 100,000 roubles. The composer himself was the soloist with the Beethoven Quartet — an ensemble which from now onwards and despite changes of personnel, was to be closely associated with his chamber music. 'Lyrically lucid, human and simple,' was Pravda's comment.

War broke out, and in the first few months Russia, in her state of military unpreparedness, suffered incredible losses and cruel reprisals at the hands of the invader. The swift Nazi advance reached the gates of Moscow, led to the occupation of Kiev and the encirclement of Leningrad whose heroic 872 day siege became the wonder of the world. Shostakovich volunteered for war service but was not accepted. (As Rabinovich says, this was 'not only on

НАПОЛЕОН ПОТЕРПЕЛ ПОРАЖЕНИЕ.
ТО ЖЕ БУДЕТ И С ЗАЗНАВШИМСЯ
ГИТЛЕРОМ!
1812г
ДОГО
ВОР
КУКРЫН

Soviet War Poster. 'Napoleon was smashed — the same fate is in store for the arrogant Hitler!' The Kukryniksy, 1941. An appeal to the Soviet citizen's historic pride. (SCR)

The composer on Fire Duty at the Leningrad Conservatoire, 1941 (Novosti)

account of his poor eyesight'.) Instead, he was given a post as fire fighter in the brigade attached to the Conservatoire and continued his duties as a composer, throwing himself into the task of organising concerts and writing war songs for the benefit of troops at the Front and the people at home. (These war songs — a genre which belonged to the mass song tradition in Soviet Russia — were collected in many volumes and some of them attained a stirring popularity comparable with Rouget de Lisle's *Marseillaise* of 1792.)

Shostakovich's seventh symphony, completed in evacuation at Kulbyshev in December 1941 and dedicated to the city of Leningrad, is the most highly documented symphony ever to have been composed. It seems that again Shostakovich wished to encompass the theme of Lenin, but the outbreak of war turned his thoughts in an entirely new direction. What follows is a brief chronological documentation of the work which made Shostakovich's name famous to a whole world at war.

Leningrad Radio, 1st September 1941. Shostakovich in a broadcast to the people:

Soviet musicians, my dear and numerous brothers-in-arms, my friends! Remember that our art is threatened by an immense danger. Let us

At work on the seventh symphony in Leningrad. (Novosti)

defend our music, let us work honestly and unselfishly . . . An hour ago I finished the score of the second movement of a new, large-scale symphonic work . . . If I succeed in completing the third and fourth movements of this work, it will be my seventh symphony.

From the war-time diary of Bogdanov-Berezovsky, 17th September 1941:

Tonight we went to Shostakovich. Twice he played for us two movements of his new symphony (the Seventh). He told us of the overall plan. The impression we all had was tremendous. Miraculous is the process of synchronisation, of instantaneous creative reaction to the surrounding experiences, clad in a complex and large form with no hint of 'belittling of the genre' . . . While he played there was an air raid. The composer suggested that we continue the music; only his family went to the shelter . . .

Later the same month, Shostakovich in a conversation with his friend and biographer Rabinovich:

In the development of the first movement war breaks suddenly into the peaceful life, I did not want to build up a naturalistic episode. The recapitulation is a funeral march, a deeply tragic episode, a mass requiem — the ordinary people honour the memory of their heroes. At first I badly wanted to have words to this part. I almost set about writing them

Autograph of the first page of Symphony No. 7, dedicated to the City of Leningrad (Reprinted by permission of Lawrence and Wishart Ltd)

myself. Then I decided to manage without words and I'm glad of it. Music is more expressive. Then comes a still more tragic episode: the common sorrow is followed by personal sorrow, of a mother, perhaps. It is sorrow so deep that no tears are left. Further, there is another lyrical fragment expressing the apotheosis of life, sunshine — at first I thought I would complete the symphony in one movement. The end of the movement is bright and lyrical, the intimate love of man for others like himself. Enough of this talk about the dead. Conversations, walks . . . Only the final bars bring a distant rumble: the war is not over.

The first performance in Moscow of the seventh symphony, March 1942 (Novosti)

Première, Palace of Culture, Kuibyshev, 3rd March 1942:

He seemed to suffer agonies during that first performance. The audience insisted on seeing him before it began, and he stood up on the platform, rigid and unsmiling. And when, after it was over, there were enthusiastic clamors for the composer, the grim young man once more climbed up to the platform, looking as if he were going to be hanged.

Moscow Première, end of March 1942:

It was performed in the afternoon, for in that troubled spring of 1942 Moscow concerts were held in daylight hours. During the performance an air-raid alert was sounded in the city. Just before the finale a man in uniform appeared on the stage next to the conductor and tried to stop the concert. Nobody left for the shelter. The symphony continued. After the eighteen-minute finale the man in uniform appeared again and appealed to the public in words that had become usual in those days: 'An air alert has been sounded.' He was answered by shouts of 'We know!' and the endless ovation continued,

Leningrad Première, 9th August 1942. (City under siege) Bogdanov-Berezovsky Diary:

Exciting sight of the hall, festive as of old, in its pristine white, the gold and the dark red, with its faultless architectural proportions . . . The hall is fancifully lit by the large crystal candelabras . . . In the audience, all — or nearly all — the representatives of the musical life of besieged Leningrad — composers, opera artists, pedagogues . . . many soldiers and officers who came with their automatic weapons directly from the front line. The orchestra was reinforced by army musicians temporarily on leave for this occasion: the score demands eight horns, six trumpets, six trombones, an enormous battery of percussion.

Poster advertising two performances of the seventh symphony in Leningrad, 15th and 16th August 1942 (Novosti)

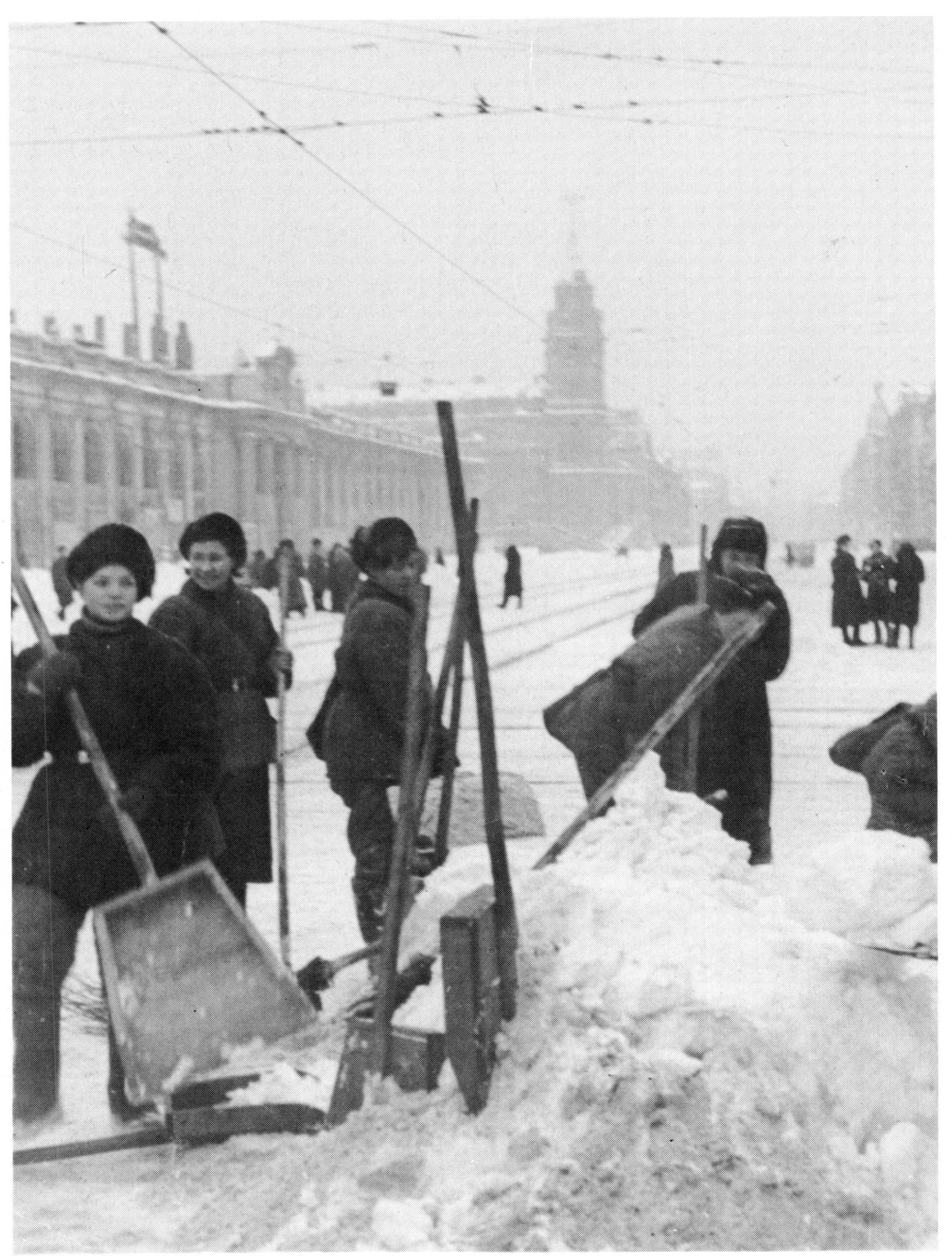

Women clearing the streets of snow during the siege of Leningrad (SCR)

> With excitement we hear the first sounds of the unison theme in the strings . . . Quite new for me were the last two movements written by Shostakovich after his departure from Leningrad . . . One cannot speak of an impression made by the symphony. It was, not an impression, but a staggering experience. This was felt not only by the listeners but also by the performers who read the music sheets as if they were reading a living chronicle about themselves . . .

The symphony became a symbolic cult. The score was sent on microfilm to the United States where in July 1942 it received its first performance in the Western Hemisphere in New York under the direction of Arturo Toscanini, leading to more than sixty performances in the USA as well as performances in Great Britain, Australia and Latin America.

After the war the symphony fell into neglect and has only recently been taken up by orchestras and conductors as more than a war time pièce d'occasion. England during the war was no place for Mahlerian symphonists — as Ernest Newman's wisecrack on its inordinate length testified. ('The position of the symphony on the musical map of the future will be located between so many

Leningrad during siege — a scene in the Nevsky Prospekt (SCR)

degrees longitude and so many degrees platitude'.) A postcript to the popular, 'optimistic' conception of the work has recently been provided by the composer himself in the Volkov memoirs:

> The Seventh Symphony became my most popular work. It saddens me, however, that people don't always understand what it's about; yet everything is clear in the music. Akhmatova wrote her *Requiem*, and the Seventh and Eighth symphonies are my requiem.

There is truth in this reported saying of the elderly composer. For (as in the fifth symphony) there is much music of a dark, overcast character amidst the more heroic affirmations. One could point to the grim climax of the first movement, or the whole of the granite-like third movement, or the Mahler-like lamentations and groans before the final peroration. A long symphony like the seventh tends to be remembered for its more obvious appeal, and the heroic martial tone in this symphony constitutes its great hold on audiences — especially those of beleaguered Russia and war-torn Europe of those days. But in the dark pages of his seventh symphony Shostakovich was remembering possibly even darker times before the war, when the enemy was unseen. As Akhmatova wrote about this pre-war Russia of Stalin's purges:

> *Yes — it's the hangman and the gibbet*
> *That set the poet's earthly scene;*
> *We keep our hairshirts on exhibit*
> *We walk with tapers, and we keen*

An amusing family anecdote from the days of the rehearsals for the first performance was related by Nina Shostakovich, who told of the young Maxim having to be removed from the scene because of his over-vigorous conducting of his father's symphony. In view of Maxim's own development into a leading exponent of his father's music from the rostrum, this incident is not without significance.

* * *

The Russian nation, 'that great and tragic people', overcame the Nazi aggressor. As in the days of Napoleon's retreat from Moscow, the weather and the sheer growing heroic fortitude of the Russian army were more than a match for them. There was much to avenge, and the Germans were not spared in a cruelly triumphant defeat. There can have been little sympathy for the shaven troops who were forced to parade down the Nevsky Prospekt in Leningrad, and in Moscow. One can see it on the faces of the street urchins who followed them. As the battles were won — at Stalingrad and at Kursk — the mood of the people changed from despair to dogged optimism and grim determination. Alexander Werth was in Leningrad in September 1943 when the siege was almost over. Comrade Semyonov, a factory director, recounted to him the mood of his workers when the siege was at its height, contrasting it with the present time:

> When they started bombing us in a big way in October 1941 our workers fought for the factory more than they fought for their own houses. There was one night when we had to deal with three hundred incendiaries in the factory grounds alone. Our people were putting the fires out with a sort of concentrated rage and fury; like a thousand squirrels they rushed around, putting out the flames. They had realised by then that they were in the front line — and that was all. No more shelters. Only small children were taken to shelters, and old grannies. And then, one day in December, in twenty degrees of frost, we had all our windows blown out by a bomb, and I thought to myself: 'No, we really can't go on. Not till the spring. We can't go on in this temperature, and without light, without water, and almost without food.' And yet, somehow — we didn't stop. A kind of instinct told us that we mustn't — that it would be worse than suicide.

In the midst of so much destruction, human misery and fortitude, Shostakovich's creative work continued. The Leningrad Symphony — was succeeded two years later by the eighth. In the days of the turning fortunes of war, it proved more difficult to come to terms with since it spoke in less heroic accents than its predecessor. It is a reflection on 'the pity and terror of war' rather than an inspiring exhortation. How else to account for the long cor anglais solo after the embattled climax of the first movement, or the two cruel and macabre scherzos with their mechanical rhythms which form the centre, or the numbed reflections on a grim theme which follow? About the finale, Shostakovich wrote that it was, 'an attempt to look into the future, into the post-war epoch. Everything evil and ugly will disappear. The beautiful will triumph.'

In between the two symphonies the composer had begun work on a strangely untopical operatic project which he abandoned. He was attracted again to Gogol, to a short story *The Gamblers* which suggests an impulse to re-invoke the old mocking fantasy of *The Nose*. What a pity it was not completed! It is about a pack of marked cards called by a woman's name, Adelaida Ivanovna, and apparently Shostakovich (in a manner which would have met with the shade of Meyerhold's approval) was to cast it for male actors/singers only. To have even conceived of such 'Meyerholdism' in music in 1942 shows the extent to which 'Socialist Realism' seemed to have loosened its grip in the war years. Why was it not completed? According to Volkov, Shostakovich had this to say:

Shostakovich with a group of his students at the Leningrad Conservatoire, 1943. 'Every mark of talent in his pupils is a sincere pleasure to him and he lends a ready ear to each student or young musician who comes to him for advice or aid'.
Martynov. (Novosti)

But when I got past ten pages, I stopped. What was I doing? First of all, the opera was becoming unmanageable, but that wasn't the important thing. The important thing was — who would put on this opera? The subject wasn't heroic or patriotic. Gogol was a classic, and they didn't perform his works anyway. . . . They would say that Shostakovich was making fun, mocking art . . .

Shostakovich had now settled permanently in Moscow where he had been appointed Professor of Composition at the Conservatoire. His ties with Leningrad — personal, creative, official — remained, none the less, close. His mother still lived there, first performances of his works continued to take place there, and he represented the City on the board of the Union of Soviet Composers. Later, in 1945, he was to resume his teaching at Leningrad. To some extent, the duality of Shostakovich's position as a composer is mirrored in the duality of Moscow and Leningrad. Moscow, the official seat of Soviet government and deposed Leningrad, the Tsarist 'window on the West'; Moscow, the city of Stalin's brash new prestige projects and Leningrad, the home of baroque splendours and rococo elegance; Moscow the emblem of pre-Tsarist Slav culture and Russian isolation from the West and Leningrad, the cosmopolitanised European city. (There is even evidence, as Ronald Hingley has pointed out, that Stalin's paranoia had led to a persecution of Leningrad intellectuals and politicians. After the assassination of Kirov, Governor of Leningrad, in 1934 'some forty thousand Leningraders were deported to the Arctic or Siberia. . . . He not only purged it again, still more severely in the late 1930's but was to do so yet again through a massacre of its notables, termed the Leningrad Affair, in 1949.')

Three important works belong to the second stage of the war years. Two of them were performed together by Shostakovich and members of the Beethoven Quartet at a concert in the Leningrad Philharmonic Hall on 14th November, 1944. These were the Piano Trio No.2, Op.67 and the Second String Quartet. The Piano Trio is a work of deep significance in the composer's autobiography. Firstly, it was dedicated to the memory of his close friend, I. I. Sollertinsky, who had died in February that year in evacuation with the Leningrad Philharmonic, of which he was the artistic director. In 1946, on the second anniversary of Sollertinsky's death, Shostakovich had this to say in honour of his dead friend:

> Sollertinsky was a clear and perfect example of a humanist artist, a scholar with great understanding in the sphere of the history of the arts, literature, philosophy and general history, a great music teacher and a clear thinker when dealing with scientific and philosophical concepts.

Shostakovich's Trio testifies to the depth and seriousness of a friendship that had begun in 1927. Another (and possibly linked) stimulus to the writing of this Trio had been the disclosure in the wake of the Nazi retreat of Jewish death camps run by the Nazis. Hitler's genocide policy towards Jews had been concealed from the Russians since the pre-war days of Stalin's pact with Germany: the discovery of atrocities against Russian Jews at Majdanek and Treblinka came as a profound shock. The last movement of the Trio — a sinister dance — is said to have been inspired by reports of how the Nazis made their victims dance on their graves before execution.

No less serious a work was the second string quartet — a quartet as elaborate and grandly conceived as the first had been simple and modestly proportioned. Here begins the composer's interest in the individual personality of his players, for this quartet is a virtuoso piece in every respect, with Beethoven once again as a clear stylistic model.

We have already mentioned Shostakovich's young son, Maxim, in connection with rehearsals for the Leningrad Symphony. (Both children had been very excited during preparations for the first performance at Kuibyshev.) His daughter, Galya, re-enters the musical scene shortly afterwards as a young beginner pianist. In the winter of 1944/45 her father promised to write her a set of piano pieces, a new one to be given each time she had learnt to play the one he had just written for her. The result was the *Children's Notebook,* Op.69 — six little pieces (March, Waltz, The Bear, Funny Story, Sad Story, Clockwork Doll) which Galya performed shortly afterwards at a concert given by the Children's Music Section of the Union of Soviet Composers. A charming photograph from that time shows father looking on as Galya displays her skill in the little suite. (One might add that the Union took their duties to the young very seriously, which was in the educating tradition of the early post-Revolutionary years. In 1935 there had been a particularly interesting conference on Music for Children which was reported in a 73-page issue of the official journal, *Sovetskaya Muzika.)*

During these later war years, and as befitted a composer of his stature, Shostakovich and his family enjoyed a summer residence at the Composer's House of the Union of Soviet Composers near Ivanovo. Here in 'a lonely forest hut' he had worked at his eighth symphony, his second piano trio and quartet, and here, too, he finished the ninth symphony in the summer of 1945. The first movement had taken him a month because of his Conservatoire work but in the peace of his summer retreat the remaining four movements were completed in the same length of time.

In 1944 his friend and biographer, D. Rabinovich, discussed with him the symphony that was to follow the eighth, because it seemed that the eighth required a successor to form a triptych complementary to that contemplative work and the 'active' seventh. 'Yes', Shostakovich had said 'I'm already thinking about the next symphony, the Ninth. I would like to write it for a chorus and solo singers as well as an orchestra if I could find suitable material for the book and if I were not afraid that I might be suspected of wanting to draw immodest analogies'. (ie with Beethoven's ninth, the Choral Symphony). There were other considerations too. With the war drawing to a close, the ninth symphony of Shostakovich would be expected to be worthy of Stalin and the victorious Russian people. 'I confess', Shostakovich said to Volkov, 'that I gave hope to the leader and teacher's dreams. I announced that I was writing an apotheosis. I was trying to get them off my back, but the attempt failed. When my ninth was performed, Stalin was incensed. He was deeply offended because there was no chorus, no soloists. And no apotheosis. There wasn't even a paltry dedication. It was just music, which Stalin didn't understand very well and which was of dubious content'.

Rabinovich was amongst the first to hear the new symphony which the composer played from his piano score. (It is, by the way, customary in the Soviet Union of Composers for new works to be played at the piano and discussed by colleagues before being heard in full orchestral dress.)

> We were prepared to listen to a new monumental fresco, something that we had the right to expect from the author of the Seventh and Eighth symphonies, especially at a time when the Soviet people and the whole world were still full of the recent victory over fascism. But we heard something quite different, something that at first astounded us by its unexpectedness . . . We were offered a symphony scherzo, a joke almost, one might say, a sinfonietta!

And so the trilogy was completed with this short work of 'dubious content', perhaps the most anti-heroic ninth symphony since Beethoven. Stalin felt let down by his court composer whose independence he was soon to curb according to well tried techniques of denigration.

Earlier that year a young Russian army officer who had served his country with distinction in the war against Nazi Germany had been arrested in an East Prussian village for allegedly making derogatory remarks about Stalin. He was one of thousands who suffered under the leader's post-war drive to reaffirm 'Socialism in One Country' and eliminate Western influence. The name of that young officer — Alexander Solzhenitsyn.

Chapter 10

Zdhanov and the second reprimand (1946–1953)

But woe betide that nation whose literature is interrupted by the use of force.

Alexander Solzhenitsyn.

The same year that Shostakovich produced his ninth symphony, Mikhail Mikhaylovich Zoshchenko, a 49 year old author of a satirical turn and a friend of the composer, had published a short story called 'The Adventures of a Monkey' which, we can be sure, Shostakovich read with interest and amusement. In it Zoshchenko implied that life for his monkey in the confines of a zoo was better than life 'outside bars' for the Soviet citizen. Zoshchenko, who had been incurring official disapproval for some time, soon found himself and his story singled out for public disgrace. Together with the Leningrad poetess, Anna Akhmatova, (whose family had suffered execution and imprisonment at the hands of the régime) he was savagely attacked for his 'bourgeois degeneracy' in a resolution of the Central Committee on August 14th, 1946. His case was discussed further by the new post-war cultural boss, Andrei Zhdanov — Stalin's right hand man, who was to give his name to a cultural purge no less extreme than the political Yezhovshchina before the war. Zhdanov denounced Zoshchenko as 'accustomed to mocking at Soviet life, Soviet conditions, and Soviet people, while disguising his mockery under a mask of empty entertainment and fatuous facetiousness.' There was no lack of evidence for Zhdanov's accusations — and it went back a long time. In 1922 Zoshchenko had belonged to a young literary group called 'The Serapion Brothers'. Since manifestos were in fashion they had published their own unfashionable credo which included the following highly un-Soviet statement: 'We do not write for propaganda. Art is real, like life itself. And, like life itself, it has neither goal nor meaning; it exists because it cannot help existing.' Such sentiments, unpopular enough in certain circles in 1922, could no longer remain unpunished in Stalin's post-war Russia. As for Akhmatova, her 'pessimism and 'individualism', her escape into a world of private emotions, were considered to be equally despicable. It was suggested by Zhdanov that these two literary figures, aided and abetted by the editors of the literary journals *Zvezda* and *Leningrad* which published their work, were corrupting the youth of Leningrad through their writings. Such literature, it was affirmed, belonged to the Imperial era of St Petersburg and the statue of the Bronze Horseman rather than that of Lenin's new and sacred dispensation.

Zhdanov was a highly educated, capable and ruthless man who had been in charge of the defence of Leningrad during the Nazi

Andrei Zhdanov, in charge of Stalin's cultural purges (Novosti)

siege of that city. As Alexander Werth pointed out, this same Zhdanov had, at one stage of the siege, taken the tough decision to let civilians starve if need be in order to provide his military forces with sufficent food. He was Stalin's most trusted aide (his posthumous reputation, incidentally, survived de-Stalinisation) and an articulate spokesmen in framing his chosen victims, formulating policy and presiding over its implementation. He could manipulate the cultural bureaucracy with a politician's cunning and, what is more, display in so doing an extremely plausible knowledge of what was going on in literature and the arts.

This cultural purge which he masterminded was an internal reflection of Stalin's post-war foreign policy: the re-affirmation (after war-time relaxations) of Communism as a political force in implacable opposition to Western Capitalism, and the drive to extend Soviet Russia's sphere of influence in Eastern Europe. The Berlin Wall dividing East from West Germany was a stark symbol of the Iron Curtain, separating Soviet Russia and its satellite countries from the so-called 'free' world. East and West began the arms race and strove to maintain the 'balance of power' through military supremacy. In 1949 Russia was to explode its first atomic device: possession and development of the 'nuclear deterrent' became a central issue in the military strategy of each side. The word 'Peace' became something of an ideological weapon in those days on both sides of the Iron Curtain, and Culture was pressed into its service.

Having dealt briskly with literature, theatre and film in turn, Comrade Zhdanov was soon to address himself to music. 1947 was the 30th anniversary of the Revolution, and it seems that composers were not taking their duty to the State as seriously as the occasion warranted. Shostakovich had produced a piece which amounted to little more than a medley of tunes by other composers; Prokofiev wrote a Festive Poem and Cantata *Flourish, Mighty Land,* which had occupied him rather less than his latest (seventh) symphony; while Khachaturian's salute was a 'Symphony-Poem' for symphony orchestra reinforced by organ and no less than fifteen trumpets which Werth described as a 'noisy, bombastic tour de force'. The 'big three' were sitting targets for Zhdanov — the time had come for a shake-up in the musical world.

Zhdanov had, suggests Werth, a 'particular spite' against Shostakovich who

> was too subtle, too delicate a personality to tolerate in Moscow, 1948. The fact that he was completely Russian, and completely Soviet, having spent all his conscious life under the Soviet system, and having scarcely

Shostakovich with the conductor, Yevgeny Mravinsky, and the violinist David Oistrakh, two of his closest colleagues in the performance of his music (Novosti)

ever been abroad, made it all the worse. Moreover, Zhdanov had a feeling that Shostakovich, though completely Russian, was also a typical product of Leningrad — a city that he, Zhdanov, had saved from the Germans but which he always suspected of being too independent-minded and rebellious at heart. That delicate boyish face, with its pale blue eyes that seemed to know so much, was irritating. It is perhaps no accident that the Central Committee's 1946 Reform of Literature should have started with Zhdanov's attack on the Leningrad writers.

It was, in fact, the work of a composer of the second rank by the name of Muradeli which provided Zhdanov with an appropriate

The family man. Shostakovich with his son, Maxim, and daughter Galya, in 1947 (Novosti)

opening theme for his attack on the current state of musical affairs. This unfortunate composer had written an opera which was intended to flatter Stalin's native Georgia but which had badly misfired in its choice of subject, since it glorified a pre-war Commissar who had died in Stalin's purges, presumably with the connivance of the Soviet leader. Stalin himself had attended a performance of this opera in December 1947 and, as in the case of Shostakovich's *Lady Macbeth* in 1935, had not approved. In his opening speech at a three day conference of composers over which he presided in January 1948 Zhdanov began by referring to this event:

Recently the Central Committee attended a pre-view of Muradeli's new opera, 'The Great Fellowship'. You realise how keenly interested we all were in this new Soviet opera, after an interval of more than ten years, in the course of which no new Soviet operas were produced. Unfortunately our hopes were not fulfilled. The new opera did not prove a success. Why was that? . . .

First, as regards its music. It has not a single melody one can remember. The music does not 'register' with the listener. The rather large and rather well-qualified audience of about 500 people did not react to a single passage in the opera . . . What one found depressing was the

Vano Muradeli — his opera *The Great Fellowship* was the subject of a forced self confession at the 1948 Conference (Novosti)

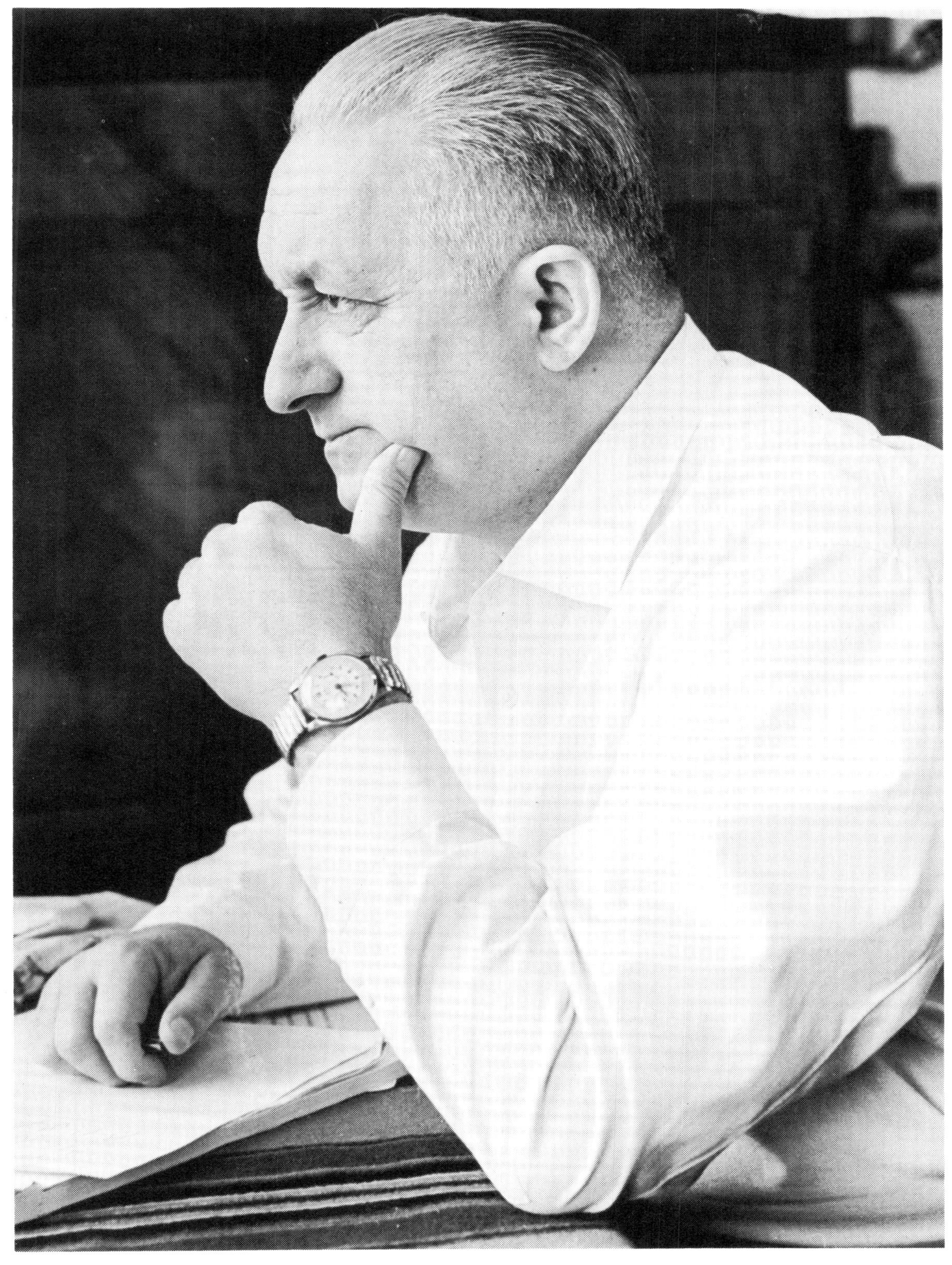

lack of harmony, the inadequacy of the musical expression of the characters' emotions, the frequent cacophonous passages . . . The orchestra is poorly used. Most of the time only a few instruments are used, and then, at unexpected moments, the whole orchestra suddenly starts blaring. During lyrical moments the drums suddenly burst in, while the heroic moments are accompanied by sad, elegiac music. And, although the opera deals with the peoples of the Northern Caucasus, during an interesting period of their history, when the Soviet Regime was being established there, the music is alien to the folk music of these peoples . . .

After recalling that this was the second conference to be held on Muradeli's opera (in the first there had been an ugly row between Stalin and the Chief Administrator of the Bolshoi Theatre who had mounted the production attended by the Central Committee), Zhdanov referred to Muradeli's blaming his 'faults' on his Conservatoire training and the critics. It was, Muradeli had maintained, his senior colleagues in music who had encouraged him to forget the classics and 'be up to date.'

'Let us try to find out whether all this is true or not' Zhdanov continued. 'This is all the more important as the faults of Muradeli's opera are very like the mistakes which, in the past, marked Comrade Shostakovich's opera, *Lady Macbeth of Mtensk* . . .' After quoting from Pravda's article of January 1936 on Shostakovich's opera, *Chaos instead of Music* (which, as we have already mentioned, is thought to have been the work of Zhdanov himself) he went on to suggest that 'what was condemned by the Party in 1936 is still going strong'. In conclusion he stated:

'If the Central Committee is wrong in defending realism and our classical heritage, then please say so openly', . . . 'what form of government exists in the Composers' Union, and its Organisational Committee? Is this form of government democratic, based on creative discussion, criticism and self criticism? Or is it all more like an oligarchy, where everything is run by a small group of composers, and their faithful retainers — I mean music critics of the boot-licking kind — and where everything is millions of miles away from real creative discussion, criticism and self criticism'.

The stage was thus set for a three day discussion in which the composing fraternity was to be set at each other's throats. It was clear that a small group of 'élitist' composers, with Shostakovich and Prokofiev at their head, was to be the chief scapegoat in this shake-up, and following a prepared speech of recantation by Muradeli promising to amend his ways, colleagues spoke for their allotted time span — some (like those in the light music camp) only too happy to sink their teeth into the officially sanctioned victims, some inclined to sit on the fence, others to introduce red herrings, and a few dignified, thoughtful and restrained in their speeches. Since music had to be 'accessible' — Zhdanov's message was clear enough — certain composers had to watch their step. And these composers were actually named in Zhdanov's final summing up — Shostakovich, Prokofiev, Khachaturian, Popov, Kabalevsky, Shebalin, with Shaporin thrown in by a voice from the floor for good measure. And, naturally, the bigger the names the more responsibility they had to carry for this state of affairs.

At the end of the conference Shostakovich spoke for himself and all serious and responsible composers when he criticised Muradeli for blaming 'other people and outside circumstances far too much for his failure'. After stating that 'every composer must first and foremost hold himself responsible for his work and his failures' he praised the wide front along which Soviet music appeared to be advancing. His final words — modest, sincere, dutiful, submissive — give no idea of the state of his personal feelings but they have a sad ring: he had learnt how, in the words of an old Russian proverb, to 'kiss but spit'.

In my work I have had many failures, even though, throughout my composer's career, I have always thought of the People, of my listeners,

Tikhon Khrennikov. He became Chairman of the Composer's Union after Zhdanov's shake-up. (Novosti)

of those who reared me; and I always strove that the People should accept my music. I have always listened to criticism, and have always tried to work harder and better. I am listening to criticism now, and shall continue to listen to it, and shall accept critical instruction . . .

I think that our three days' discussion will be of the greatest value, especially if we closely study Comrade Zhdanov's speech. I, no doubt like others, should like to have the text of his speech. A close study of this remarkable document should help us greatly in our work.

* * *

Zhdanov's conference and the subsequent decree had its intended effect. Shostakovich and his colleagues at the head of the Composers' Union were replaced by a vigorous young composer-administrator called Khrennikov who lost no time in making a clean sweep. For Shostakovitch it meant also severe restrictions on his work as a professor at the Leningrad and Moscow Conservatories and — what seems much more sinister — his deployment by Stalin's bureaucracy as a cultural emblem at the various International Peace conferences which were then in vogue. Was it, perhaps, a slyly conceived punishment that the officially dethroned Soviet genius whose music was, once again, in doubtful odour, should be sent as a member of cultural delegations to foreign countries and obliged to deliver official speeches in praise of the Soviet régime? The photographs of the composer engaged in this work do not suggest the face and posture of a man enjoying himself. During these years he found himself chosen as a delegate to conferences in Warsaw (1950), Vienna (1952) and — most publicised of all — the USA in March, 1949. One may well ask why his successor at the Composers' Union, Khrennikov, was not chosen for what amounted to an ideological confrontation between East and West. (Shostakovich's official USA speech was overtly political and anti-bourgeois in tone.) But the irony was that Dmitri Shostakovich, branded at home as 'formalist' and 'bourgeois degenerate' was the one composer (apart from Prokofiev, who was both ailing and — because of his Westernised background — unsuitable) known to the world at large as a Soviet genius. In the eyes of the West he became something of an enigma — a great composer whose music spoke for humanity trapped in a political web as a kind of willing victim of the régime. Nor did his trials and tribulations finish when he got home, for he was naturally pestered by the Soviet journals to publish his (perforce very superficial) impressions of life in the 'decadent West', with which he obliged more or less willingly. It obviously went down well in Moscow and Leningrad for him to tell the readers of *Novy Mir* that he was greeted at the airport by a friendly reporter who, hailing him as 'Shosty', asked him whether he preferred blondes or brunettes. But he was a Soviet composer and family man, not a journalist, and one can imagine that such work was little more than a time-consuming chore after an exhausting and personally distasteful trip.

These were the years of 'Prestige Projects' glorifying the Stalin régime, epitomised in such a building as that of Moscow State University — a 'wedding cake' construction 32 stories high and topped with a spire — which took four years to complete. But such

'Wedding Cake' architecture of the Stalin Era — Moscow State University (SCR)

projects hid, as it were, a cultural desert. The creative arts were stifled, and artists had to come to terms with the situation as best they may. Some major figues were spared the problems of survival. Both Eisenstein, the great film director (who had also been denounced in 1946) and Prokofiev were to die prematurely — Eisenstein in 1948 at the age of 51 and Prokofiev, who had collaborated with him in some great films, in 1953, aged 61. There were other irreparable losses to music at this time. In 1949 the great academician Boris Asafiev died, a writer and theorist of towering intellect who had supported Shostakovich and influenced successive generations of Soviet musicians, the brilliant Sollertinsky amongst them. (Asafiev had been a great admirer of Shostakovich, of whom he had once said 'One cannot but be proud of a talent, so unique, so nervously original, and so universally significant . . .'.) And the following year Miaskovsky, composer of no less than twenty-seven symphonies, who had not escaped censure in the recent conference for his 'formalistic errors' also died, a broken and embittered old man who had sincerely come to terms with the Soviet régime but in so doing had not compromised his artistic integrity. To set against this impoverishment in Soviet musical life, there was a rising generation of executant artists — the cellist Rostropovich (b. 1927), the pianist Richter (b. 1914) and the violinist, David Oistrakh, for

The distinguished symphonist, Miaskovsky, who together with Shostakovich and other outstanding figures in Soviet music, was pilloried in 1948 (Novosti)

whom Shostakovich wrote his first violin concerto, the first of the 'performance postponed' works following the Zhdanov conference.

To continue writing his serious works and withhold their performance until times were more favourable to their reception — this became Shostakovich's way of preserving his creative integrity following his second fall from grace in 1948. He was, after all, used to such a device. In 1934 he had withdrawn his fourth symphony and the work still awaited performance. (That he contemplated its eventual presentation and continued to take an interest in its existence is shown by his preparing a version for two pianos in 1946.) Now that there was clearly no chance for anything in music but Soviet propaganda of the most immediately accessible kind he dutifully intensified his activity as a film composer and writer of appropriate celebratory cantatas, of which the fresh and tuneful *Song of the Motherland* of 1952 is an especially attractive offering. At the same time he continued to work on the larger scale, in the symphonic first violin concerto mentioned above and later in the two string quartets, Nos. 4 and 5, both of which must be ranked as serious, highly individual creations. In the symphonically conceived fifth quartet in particular, there is not a trace of 'writing down to an audience'. On the contrary, the musical argument is sustained and does not shirk the kind of fierce inner struggle for stabilisation that is always characteristically at odds with happy endings in his best work. No doubt the dissonances of this piece would have been considered in Zhdanov's words, 'violations of the rules of normal human hearing . . . bad, disharmonious music' with 'a bad effect on the psycho-physiological activity of man'. But neither Zhdanov (who had in any case died in August, 1948) nor Stalin (whose time was now short) were to hear a note of it.

In both the violin concerto (second movement) and the opening of the fifth quartet we encounter for the first time a motto theme which incorporates the composer's musical signature, the letters DSCH derived from the German spelling of the composer's name and its German note equivalents, the pitches D, E flat, C and B. That this theme begins to make itself heard at a time when a composer cultivated individuality in public at his peril is a small but telling sign of Shostakovich's refusal to kow-tow in his art to the dictates of Stalin. And in the tenth symphony, composed immediately after the death of Stalin, that musical motif becomes the triumphant motto of the entire symphony. We notice in these works the beginning of that tendency in the composer to treat all his music as an inter-related whole, using figures and motifs to which one is tempted to attach extra-musical significance. (In this respect he resembles Schumann.) Another work, composed but withheld from performance at this time, was the Song Cycle *From Jewish Folk-Poetry* of 1948. In it Shostakovich identifies with the sufferings of ordinary Jewish people before the revolution and, in the last three songs, dutifully rejoices with them in their new found happiness in Soviet Russia.

Shostakovitch has said that 'In our day and age any person with pretensions to decency cannot be anti-Semitic'. He recalled how these songs came into being.

Once after the war I was passing a bookshop and saw a volume with Jewish songs. I was always interested in Jewish folk-lore, and I thought the book would give the melodies, but it contained only the texts. It seemed to me that if I picked out the several texts and set them to music, I would be able to tell the fate of the Jewish people. It seemed an important thing to do, because I could see anti-Semitism growing all round me.

The first performance (1955) of the withheld 'Songs from Jewish Folk Poetry', composed in 1948, with the composer at the piano. (Novosti)

He took no chances in allowing these settings to be heard. It was known that Stalin's make-up contained in it an element of anti-Semitism. As Ronald Hingley has pointed out

In the post-war Stalinist period . . . the campaign against 'cosmopolitans' was given a calculated anti-Semitic twist, though Jews were prominent amongst the persecutors as well as the persecuted. On 12th August 1952 Stalin had a number of prominent Jews, including Jewish writers, executed on suspicion of planning to turn the Crimea into a Jewish national home. He was also planning to 'frame' certain doctors, chiefly Jewish, on charges of assassinating influential patients by medical means, and to make this the basis for a new nationwide purge.

That Shostakovich could be roused to protest and anger at anti-Semitism we shall see in later works. Meanwhile it is significant that Stalin's post-war régime induced the first of these outcries.

The composer's secret form of protest was, of course, not known at this time by colleagues such as Pasternak in whom the spirit of dissent was already growing. He could only judge from what appeared to be a grovelling conformity in Shostakovich's behaviour. In her memoirs, Olga Ivinskaya recalls

When the campaign against Dmitri Shostakovitch was launched, BL (Boris Pasternak) decided he must write him a letter to cheer him up. He drafted something and showed it to me. But I remember saying: 'Wait a little before you send it. You'll see: tomorrow he'll recant and start beating his breast'.

But BL sent it off without telling me. How mortified he was when my words turned out to be all too true. I recall a very characteristic comment by BL: 'Oh Lord, if only they knew how to keep silent at least! Even that would be an act of courage!'

During the whole period under review, only two serious works by the composer were heard. One was at the very beginning of the 'Zhdanovschina' (before it had touched music), on 16th December 1948, when Moscow heard the third string quartet for the first time, dedicated to and played by the Beethoven Quartet. At this première it produced a great impression. Rabinovich, who was at the performance, recalled the words of a famous Russian pianist, Professor Konstantin Igumnov, on that occasion.

Do you know, that man sees and feels life a thousand times more profundly than all of us, the other musicians put together.

And Alexander Werth, discussing the work in the context of the

The Beethoven Quartet in a performance of one of Shostakovich's most acclaimed works, the Piano Quintet, with the composer at the piano. (Novosti)

Zhdanov Conference (where it had been branded by one speaker as 'formalist') had said

There is undoubtedly a feeling of profound tragedy, bordering on pessimism in his wonderful third quartet, where the personal anguish of a modern Soviet man is, first, fitted into the patterns of a Bach-like Largo, and, in the finale, into that of a Beethoven Rondo.

The other work was a collection of Preludes and Fugues which had been inspired by the playing of a Soviet pianist who had won the first prize playing the whole of Bach's 48 Preludes and Fugues at the First International Bach competition in Leipzig in 1950, commemorating the 200th anniversary of Bach's death. Tatiana Nikolayeva, who gave the work its first performance on December 23rd 1952 in Leningrad, remembered in 1974 how she became involved.

Shostakovich with the film director G. Alexandrov in 1950 during his fall from grace after the Zhdanov cultural purge of 1947. Film music became Shostakovich's official form of repentance while he continued to write 'seriously' for himself, in the hope of better times (Novosti)

In 1950 the first international Bach competition was held. It was a great occasion, in fact it was a sort of national celebration with invited guests, among whom Dmitri Dmitrievich had a special place of honour. I was then a young girl, just out of the Conservatory but I had nerve and entered for the competition and won first prize playing the whole of

Bach's 48 Preludes and Fugues. And if this then is what stimulated Shostakovich to write his own 24 Preludes and Fugues them I'm tremendously pleased.

This two volume cycle recalls a similar feat by Shostakovich's great German contemporary, Paul Hindemith who, in 1942, had written *his* successor to Bach's 48 Preludes and Fugues, the *Ludus Tonalis*. But these Preludes and Fugues of Shostakovich which have come to be much played and admired by audiences in Russia, ran ideological risks in 1950. Had not Professor Keldysh on the second day of the conference said:

> the neo-classical tendencies we find in some of our composers are derived from the West, and are a form of escapism. We cannot express Soviet reality and the feelings of Soviet Man in terms of Bach-like stylisations . . .

The old smear of 'Music for Music's sake' could always be applied in a witch hunt. It is only to be expected in such a climate of hostility that Shostakovich turned to film music as a means of professional survival. But in his 'secret' works he continued to write for less ideologically prejudiced ears, and the time was not far off when they would be heard.

Chapter 11

Death of Stalin and an artist's liberation – The Tenth Symphony (1953–1966)

If feeling fails you, vain will be your course,
And idle what you plan unless your art
Springs from the soul with elemental force
To hold its sway in every listening heart

Goethe — *Faust*

Ronald Hingley has written that Stalin's regimentation of the Arts between the years 1946 and 1952

> led to intellectual and cultural stagnation so extreme that even the authorities who imposed it, led by Stalin himself, began to show mild signs of dissatisfaction with what they had wrought.

On the same subject, Gleb Struve recalls that

> In 1952, Pravda initiated a debate about what came to be known as 'theory of conflictlessness'. Soviet writers . . . were reminded that there were still enough survivals of capitalism in the consciousness of the Soviet man, that conditions were still far from ideal in the Soviet Union, that there was enough evil in Soviet life and plenty of 'negative characters.'

Struve goes on to quote *Pravda* as saying 'We need not fear showing up our shortcomings and difficulties. We need Gogols and Shchedrins'.

Such a call, if it caught Shostakovich's eye (and party directives on literature could give useful advance warning of any changes in the general cultural climate) would perhaps have given him encouragement for the future, though it was always unwise to act too hastily.

The year 1953 began ominously enough with the so-called 'Doctors' Plot', in which nine prominent doctors (most of whom were Jewish) were arrested on charges of poisoning Soviet leaders. This was clearly a herald of further purges, but then on 25th February the accompanying press campaign of vigilance unaccountably broke off. At the beginning of March Moscow Radio began to broadcast conflicting daily bulletins about the state of Stalin's health, following an announcement that on the night of 1/2 March the leader had suffered a serious stroke. Finally, on 6th March it was announced that Stalin had died the day before and an appeal for unity and calm was made by the Party Central Committee and the Council of Ministers. After a short lying in state, eight of the most powerful political leaders (including Malenkov, Molotov, Beria and Khrushchev) carried the coffin to the Mausoleum where Stalin's embalmed body was to lie under glass next to that of Lenin.

The mood of the people, despite the outward show of grief and the obligatory poems of deification, was uneasy. The fear was that Stalinism would be replaced by something worse, but as the weeks passed 'Collective Leadership' became the new slogan and with it, amongst artists and intellectuals, an unmistakable feeling of thaw after the long Zhdanov winter.

The 'Doctors' Plot' affair was revoked. The first sign of shifts in power came with the arrest of Stalin's Chief of Police, Beria, on 10th July. (Together with certain of his accomplices he was executed on 23rd December.) 'In the late summer of 1953, after the arrest of Beria', wrote Edward Crankshaw 'everyone started singing, at first tentatively, then in a rush, as a full dawn chorus.' On the cultural front, Pravda, on 27th November, published a statement which criticised standardisation in art.

> To pattern all art on one model is to obliterate individuality . . . Socialist Realism offers boundless vistas for the creative artist and the greatest freedom for the expression of his personality, for the development of diverse art genres, trends and styles. Hence the importance of encouraging new departures in art, of studying the artist's individual style, and . . . of recognising the artist's right ot be independent, to strike out boldly on new paths.

Shostakovich had not been slow to take advantage of the change of weather brought about by Stalin's death. On 13th November the Beethoven Quartet performed in Moscow his shelved fifth string quartet — a strenuous work conceived on the large scale, with many pre-echoes of the tenth symphony. Then, on 3rd December, came the first performance of the fourth quartet, a work which contained some dark — even sinister — sayings in its suppressed and muted later parts. (The finale is a dance recalling the Jewish death dance of the Piano Trio No.2.) And on 17th December the Leningrad Philharmonic Orchestra under Mravinsky performed in the composer's home city (it was, appropriately enough, the year of Leningrad's 250th anniversary celebrations) the work which has come to be universally recog-

Leningrad celebrates. Fireworks over the Neva (SCR)

nised as perhaps his greatest, most perfect achievement — the tenth symphony. As in the case of the fifth symphony we must pause to take stock of this achievement — which became the subject of an important debate that raised in its sharpest form the issue of creative freedom and State control of Soviet Russia. It was a debate from which Shostakovich and his tenth symphony emerged victorious; but, as Boris Schwarz has pointed out, Shostakovich's right to speak as a creative individual was granted to him rather grudgingly by many of his colleagues in the debate — especially those who had thrived in the Stalin/Zhdanov dispensation.

Picc.
a2
Fl.
a2
Ob.
Cl. picc.
a2
Cl.
g.
C-fag.
D S C H
a2
Cor.
a2
ff
ff
a2
Tr-be
ff
ff
Tr-ni
e
Tuba
Timp.
T-ro
202
Archi

Shostakovich's personal motto, DSCH, as it appears at the end of the tenth symphony on horns and trumpets (Reproduced by permission of Anglo-Soviet Music Press Ltd)

Perhaps the most interesting information that has recently come to light on the tenth symphony has come from the composer himself in conversation with his friend Solomon Volkov. He told him that Stalin was depicted in the work, and that the second part, the scherzo, was a musical portrait of Stalin. This music — furious, violent, brutally percussive — could certainly be taken as the embodiment in sound of evil power, and what better candidate than Stalin for the inhuman presence thus personified?

Fadeyev, the novelist, may have paid tribute to the leader and teacher as 'the greatest humanist the world ever knew' but Pasternak was undoubtedly nearer the mark when (while allowing for his intuition) he called him a 'madman and a murderer'. We have a portrait in words of Stalin by the Petersburg poet Mandelstam (a victim of the purges in the thirties) which has been handed on to us by Olga Ivanskaya, Pasternak's mistress and confidante. It runs as follows:

We live, deaf to the land beneath us,
Ten steps away no one hears our speeches,

But where there's so much as half a conversation
The Kremlin's mountaineer will get his mention.

His fingers are fat as grubs
And the words, final as lead weights, fall from his lips,

His cockroach whiskers leer
And his top boots gleam.

Around him a rabble of thin-necked leaders —
Fawning half men for him to play with.

They whinney, purr, or whine
As he prates and points a finger,

One by one forging his laws, to be flung
Like horse shoes at the head, the eye, or the groin.

And every killing is a treat
For the broad-chested Ossete.

Shostakovich's music is a fitting complement to Mandelstam's poem and carries with it something of the same epigrammatic force and brevity.

How far is the tenth symphony a programme symphony? At the time of its first performance Shostakovich was evasive about its meaning, but there was no denial of a possible secret programme, and the work certainly seems to require interpretation. 'Authors like to say of themselves, I tried, I wanted to, etc'. the composer wrote. 'But I think I'll refrain from any such remarks. One thing I will say; in this composition I wanted to portray human emotions

II

71
Allegro ♩= 176
Piccolo
2 Flauti
I.II
3 Oboi
III
a2
ff
Clarinetto piccolo (Es)
2 Clarinetti (B)
2 Fagotti
Contrafagotto
I.II
4 Corni (F)
III.IV
I.II
3 Trombe (B)
III
3 Tromboni e Tuba
Timpani
Triangolo
Tamburo
Piatti
Cassa
Silofono
71
Allegro ♩= 176
senza sord.
Violini I
Violini II
Viole
Violoncelli
Contrabassi

The second movement of the tenth symphony — 'a musical portrait of Stalin, roughly speaking'. Shostakovich to Volkov in his memoirs. (Reproduced by permission of Anglo-Soviet Music Press Ltd)

and passions'. And in conversation with friends later who asked him if he would publish a programme he is reported to have said 'No, let them listen and guess for themselves'.

There is much room for speculation as to the 'meaning' of this symphony. Perhaps the most enigmatic movement is the third, which seems to be using a succession of themes and motives like code signals. It is here that the listener could do with a list of leitmotives and their significance in the Wagnerian sense. How does one interpret the five note call on the horn which appears twelve times in the second half of the movement? Is it a question or an affirmation? What is its relationship to DSCH, the composer's personal motto, with which it is constantly associated? The tentative dance steps of this music, with its curious amalgam of hope, joy, despair, struggle, suggest an extra-musical stimulus: perhaps the death of Stalin has given rise to this complex of emotion — relief, unease, hope for the future but doubt and fear also. The long first movement is brooding and overcast, with backward references at points of climax to an embattled motif from the bleak and tragic eighth symphony. Is this a reflection on more than twenty years of suffering on the large scale? Moreover, this movement is pervaded by a theme for cellos and basses which recalls in its brooding rise and fall the theme Liszt used in his *Faust* symphony. Is Shostakovich offering a clue to his listeners that the 'Faust' legend — man as a restless, questioning seeker after the secrets of the universe — is one of the sources of inspiration here? (It may be no mere co-incidence that Pasternak's translation of Goethe's *Faust* was published the same year.) The quick music of the finale, after a groping introduction in which the darkness is pierced by lonely cries, sounds positive and carefree enough, but it develops into a tense conflict of themes (recalling the Stalin terrors of the scherzo) before the clouds disperse at length and DSCH proclaims his vigorous supremacy in the horns and drums.

Shostakovich believed in the concept of music as an organising force, with the power of stirring specific emotions in those who listen to it. Back in 1931, in his interview with the American journalist Rose Lee, he had said that 'Beethoven's Third awakens one to the joy of struggle', that Beethoven 'wished to give new ideas to the public and rouse it to revolt against its masters'. It seems likely that in 1953 he felt that the time had come for an assertion of the artist's personality, for a renewed drive towards more truthful expression, for a rejection of the Stalin terror. Stalin's death and subsequent political events seemed to provide him with his opportunity. In a sense, the tenth is the closing work in the cycle of not three but *seven* 'war' symphonies — beginning with the fourth — composed during the Stalin era. Much of it would seem to be looking back on a time of darkness and despair, while the finale seems to offer his audience a message of hope through individual self-assertion. Such a message was in no way 'counter revolutionary'. On the contrary, Shostakovich felt this with an artist's intuition — the time was ripe for distinguishing between the social ideals of Lenin's revolution (in which he sincerely believed) and the course taken by Stalin, whom Trotsky had branded as its grave digger. While Stalin had achieved much in terms of Soviet prestige, social welfare and economic prosperity, the human cost had been too high. Shostakovich's symphony invited its original Soviet audience to consider its present position in human rather than political terms after more than two decades of terror, now that the instigator of that terror had disappeared.

The work was taken very seriously by critics and composers alike. It became a cause célèbre. A three day conference on it was held by the Composers' Union in March and April, 1954. Indeed, the debate between creative genius and the Zhdanovites was already under way before that conference took place. The January issue of Sovetskaya Muzika had included an article by Shostakovich called 'The Joy of Seeking New Ways' in which he had stated that 'In my opinion, the Union should not "protect" our composers against exploring the new, against independent movements along an unbeaten track in art . . . ' In making this appeal he had the full backing of his colleague Khachaturian who had, in an article which appeared shortly before the first performance of the tenth symphony, identified a need for greater freedom in music. All this had the appearance of a campaign in favour of 'de-Stalinisation' of the composers' bureaucracy. (What backing behind the scenes did Shostakovich and Khachaturian receive for this line of argument, one wonders?) On the other hand, in the same issue that printed Shostakovich's article there appeared another by Dzerzhinsky called 'Fight for Realistic Art'. Dzerzhinsky (whom Gerald Abraham has described as 'opera-purveyor-in-chief to Soviet Russia') possessed a compositional technique that was vastly inferior to that of Shostakovich: one cannot rule out professional envy as his motive. Be that as it may, the composer of *And Quiet flows the Don* sniped in this article at Shostakovich's recent works, including the 24 Preludes and Fugues and the Fifth String Quartet, asking somewhat speciously if Shostakovich and his colleagues were being helped sufficiently 'in their difficult struggle with the grave consequences of formalist delusions'. The 'holier than thou' implication of such an article, with its obvious aim of keeping the composer of the tenth symphony in the place allotted to him by Zhdanov, were representative of the other side of the debate on the symphony which followed on 29th March. Before the debate opened,

Stalin, whose death in 1953 inaugurated a more liberal era (SCR)

Shostakovich made a few apparently modest and self-critical remarks about his new symphony — technical remarks about parts being too short or too long — studiedly avoiding any reference to specific content or meaning. The composers and critics, however, had a good deal to say about such matters. Khachaturian had, before the conference, already written in admiring terms about the work as 'life affirming' and possessing 'deep emotional and philosophical content'. 'As a composer' he had written 'I cannot tire of admiring the dramaturgic mastery of D. Shostakovich, his ability to build a large form, to saturate each part of the symphony with movement, to constantly hold his listener in tense attention'.

At the conference, composers seemed to be in agreement about the work's musical quality but disagreed over its message. There was obviously some nervousness (both at the conference and in subsequent critical studies of the work) as to how far Shostakovich had overstepped Zhdanov's original guide lines. Thus the critic Boris Yarustovsky expressed the opinion that the work was

> the tragedy of a profoundly isolated individual. It seems that the hero of the symphony has to meet the forces of evil alone. Out of his purely personal and therefore narrow world he looks in horror at that evil and the cataclysms it wreaks and feels that he is helpless in the face of them. Such a conception of the world is very far from that which is experienced by the majority of Soviet people.

Khrennikov, too, felt that the composer's *Song of the Forests* represented 'the truth of our life' more convincingly that his Tenth Symphony. Enthusiasts for the work used such terms as 'optimistic tragedy', the end of the theory of 'conflictlessness'. Regardless of these professional clashes of opinion on the symphony, however, its author was officially honoured with the award of 'People's Artist of the USSR' in the summer of 1954. The two fellow recipients of the award were Khachaturian, and Shaporin, a veteran, unimpeachably Soviet composer of 65 who had been trained in that same Rimsky Korsakov-Steinberg school against which the younger Shostakovich had rebelled. Thus Shostakovich found himself in very respectable company indeed and his individualism vindicated.

The 'sharp and sometimes heated' debate on Shostakovich's new symphony aroused intense interest and curiosity in both the man and his music outside the Soviet Union, and we are fortunate in having a record of a personal interview with the composer by the Moscow correspondent of the New York Times which took place in August, 1954. This is how Mr Harrison E. Salisbury described Shostakovich at the interview:

Dmitri Shostakovich will be 48 years old this year. He has been composing major works for thirty years. While still giving an impression of youthfulness, he has in recent years lost that rather cherubic look which some one once described as that of 'lost rabbit'. Today Shostakovich looks blond, trim and fit, and it is easy to believe him when he says, with his eyes and face lighting up, that sport is his hobby . . .

Salisbury notices that 'seriousness and earnestness dominate Shostakovich's character,' both in conversation and in repose. He comments on his nervousness — his cigarette smoking and restless fingers, and it is evident too that although the composer is talking about himself, yet he is anxious to speak of himself as representative of the Soviet composer rather than as an individual. We have, too, a fascinating glimpse of the Shostakovich family life-style at this period. Visiting his private apartment in Mozhaisky Boulevard after the interview at the Composers' Union in Miusskaya Square Salisbury notes:

With two musicians in the family there are certain problems. But, fortunately . . . he has a large apartment of five rooms, divided in such a way that when he has the doors of his studio closed he is not bothered by any outside noises, such as the sound of his son practising on his own piano. There are four pianos in the Shostakovich household — Shostakovich has two in his studio, both Bluthners (his favourite make). His son has another and there is a fourth at their country home . . . The country house, or dacha, is about thirty miles outside Moscow and a very pleasant place indeed. There is a big garden. There is room to play volley ball, and the Klyazma River is convenient for swimming. Shostakovich does not own the dacha. He rents it from the Soviet Government . . . He is not too particular where he works — either in town or in the dacha. But, as he says, 'when the telephone gets too busy, sometimes I come out to the dacha for two or three days'. He drives a Pobeda (Victory) four-cylinder machine which cost about 14,000 rubles ($3500).

These glimpses of the composer's material circumstances are evidence of both his status and the way in which the Soviet Union looks after its creative artists. What with Ministry of Culture fees, sales of music and performance royalties, Stalin Prizes, etc., the composer was earning a very good living. Despite the bureaucratic pressures of his position and his teaching commitments (which would have increased considerably at this time of official reinstatement and recognition) he was able to take the time needed for creative work.

The interview with Harrison Salisbury confirms that free debate was now again possible amongst composers, and Shostakovich loses no opportunity to stress the advantages of his position as a Soviet composer in comparison with his Western counterpart. Salisbury reports Shostakovich's argument as follows:

International success of the tenth symphony. The composer applauds Karajan after a Moscow performance of the tenth symphony in 1971 (Novosti)

. . . the artist in the Soviet Union occupies what might be described as a 'principled' relationship to society and to the Party, whereas in the West, or so Shostakovich believes, the artist's relationship to society is haphazard. Neither the Western artist, nor his art, as Shostakovich sees them, has a 'status' in society founded upon principles. But in Russia such a status, such a relationship to State and society, and such a set of principles do exist and actually define the role of the artist.

It seems that in composing the tenth symphony Shostakovitch actually found himself in the position of expressing and influencing the new post-Stalin ideological trend towards individuality and licence to admit tragedy and conflict into a work of art. The West greeted the work with open arms. After its first performance in New York on 15th October 1954 Olin Downes wrote:

Shostakovitch, born of troubled times, has gone through much to reach this symphony. It seems to us the sure token of his arrival at the master's estate, and it should precede more scores of his growing power.

Chapter 12

Composer Laureate – a Lenin Symphony at last. Cultural thaw and a new period of creative development (1954–1966)

Russia has changed, Yesenin my friend,
but, to my mind, shedding tears is purposeless:
I hesitate to say that things are on the mend
— and to say they're worse is dangerous.

There's no end of new buildings and sputniks to spare,
but the going was rough and on the way
we lost twenty millions in the war
— and millions more in war upon the nation.

Yevtushenko — Letter to Yesenin.

Amongst the composer's closest colleagues and contemporaries, the violinist David Oistrakh — only two years his junior — emerges as a staunch and loyal supporter at this time. He had been unable to be present during the discussion on the 10th symphony, but having read a report of the proceedings in *Sovetskaya Muzika* he was moved to spring to the composer's defence in view of a reactionary contribution made by a Leningrad musicologist named Y. Kremlev. Kremlev had written that the symphony 'has no real themes, real singing, rhythmic and harmonic high-lights — the bases of realist music . . . ' To which Oistrakh replied

I am far from being an unqualified lover of Shostakovich's work. I like some of his work very much and am critically disposed to other pieces. But the 10th symphony has impressed me deeply. It has nothing in it which I cannot believe, nothing which has been written for its outward effectiveness alone. The symphony has a deeply ethical opening and great humanity, and is filled with the sincere feelings of a great artist and patriot. Its strength lies in its great dramatic effect, the sharp conflict in it and the enchanting beauty and truthfulness of its images.

After its first performance in the Great Hall of the Conservatoire I came home deeply moved and listened again to it, recorded on magnitophone during the performance. Shostakovich's 10th symphony has become one of my favourite works.

The following year Oistrakh gave the world premiere in Leningrad of the one work written during the 'Zhdanovshchina' remaining to be heard — the first violin concerto, which had had to wait seven years for its first performance. The concerto was Shostakovich's biggest piece to be composed between the third string quartet of 1949 and the 10th symphony of 1953. It is a large scale symphonic conception in four movements, sharing certain thematic ideas with the fifth quartet and the tenth symphony, including the DSCH motto. Oistrakh's enthusiasm for the piece knew no bounds and he played it may times, 'always with great enjoyment'. 'It is', he wrote 'a very attractive role that offers great opportunities, not merely for the violinist to demonstrate his virtuosity, but rather for the exposition of the most profound emotions, thoughts and moods . . . The more I learned to know the concerto, the more attentively I listened to its sounds, the more it pleased me so that I studied it with still greater enthusiasm, thought about it, lived for it . . . '

The second performance of the concerto was given by Oistrakh not in Moscow but in New York's Carnegie Hall on 29th December 1955, with Mitropoulos conducting the New York Philharmonic Orchestra. Boris Schwarz, who was at that performance recalls 'the unique experience of discovering, at the same time, a great composition and a great performer' describing how 'In response to the enthusiastic applause, Mitropoulos — in a symbolic gesture — lifted the score of the Concerto towards the audience as if to let the new work share in the ovation accorded the masterful performance'.

Amidst this public acclaim, Shostakovich's private life was overcast by the premature death of his wife Nina in late 1954 and of his mother at the age of 67 the following year. (His two children, Galya and Maxim, were in their late teens at this time of bereavement.) In memory of his first wife he later wrote the seventh string quartet, a work which remained a particular favourite with him. The dedication implies that the work had particular autobiographical associations and the content readily lends itself to such an interpretation. First comes a Haydnesque Allegro, subtle yet reflective and characterised by the composer's rhythmic motto — the anapaest, then a sad slow movement with funeral overtones, and finally a frenzied fugue calming into a gentle dance and fading reminiscences of the first movement. The sequence suggest a meditation on the life and death of its dedicatee: in much the same way as Berg's Violin Concerto was a meditation on the life and death of a deeply loved girl. Since music and life were inseparable elements for Shostakovich perhaps some such secret programme exists, but we shall never know. And the music needs no such autobiographical programme to be understood as a classically balanced expression of many moods. A more extrovert piece is the second piano concerto which he wrote to display the gifts of his son, Maxim, on his nineteenth birthday, 10th May, 1957. Maxim's performance that day gained him entrance to the Moscow State Conservatoire. The work, with its enchanting echoes of Rachmaninov in the second movement for piano and strings only, remains a firm favourite with audiences. Thus it came about that both his children were able to look back on works specially composed for them in their childhood and youth by their father — Galya on her little piano suite of 1949 and Maxim on his much more demanding concerto which, as Rabinovich says, 'shows the composer as though his own youth had returned to him'.

The composer's second marriage, to Margarita Andreyevna Kainova in 1956 was, according to Volkov, unhappy and short lived. Ten years later — in 1966 — he married for the third time, and it was his third wife, Irena Suprinskaya who supported him through the later years of increasing frailty up to the time of his death. Perhaps one day she will publish her memoirs. Meanwhile the veil on Shostakovich's closely guarded private life was rarely lifted. Not that he can have found much time for family life — composition, teaching, performances to attend, invitations abroad, acknowledgement of public honours, duties in his capacity as Soviet Russia's leading composer, speeches to deliver, articles to write. In the absence of diaries and private correspondence the biographer has to content himself with fleeting glimpses of the man as he appeared in public or in private to friends and colleagues. To such anecdotes we shall return towards the end of this chapter. Meanwhile there is no shortage of public events to report on during these momentuous years.

In 1956 Khrushchev became Party Leader in succession to Stalin and on 25th February delivered his historic speech in denunciation of his predecessor at a closed session of the 20th Conference of the Communist Party. Here was the final stage of a process of de-Stalinisation that had been going on since the death of the leader. In his speech Khrushchev referred to 'the great harm caused by the violation of the principle of collective leadership and . . . the accumulation of immense and unlimited powers in the hands of one person'. The ideological shift was towards the spirit of the early post-revolutionary decade and a replacement of Stalin's image by that of Lenin. Khrushchev quoted from Lenin's last letters about Stalin — his demand for an apology after Stalin had insulted his (Lenin's) wife: 'I consider as directed against me that which is done against my wife.' He stated that anybody differing from Stalin was 'doomed to removal from the leading collective and to subsequent moral and physical annihilation', informing the party members that during 1937–38 70% of the Central Committee members were shot. He also indicated that Kirov's murder in Leningrad (which had made way for Zhdanov) had been arranged by Stalin. He drew attention to the method of extorting confessions by torture, mentioning the case of an old Bolshevik, one Eikhe, who had written 'not being able to suffer the tortures to which I was submitted by Ushakov and Mikolaev . . . who took advantage of the knowledge that my broken ribs have not properly mended and have caused me great pain, I have been forced to accuse myself and others. Most of my confession has been suggested or dictated by Ushakov'.

Finally, he criticised Stalin's role in the war — his state of unpreparedness for the German invasion due in part to his purge of officers during 1937 to 1941. One such officer, a close friend of Shostakovich's, had been shot on Stalin's orders. His name was Tukhachevsky. As Shostakovich recalled

When Tukhachevsky insisted on increasing the number of planes and tanks, Stalin called him a hare-brained schemer. But during the war, after the first crushing defeats, Stalin caught on. It was the same with rockets. Tukhachevsky began rocketry while in Leningrad. Stalin later had all the Leningrad rocketry experts shot, and then they had to start from scratch'.

Khrushchev's speech heralded a period of political detente, individual freedom and cultural exchange such as Soviet Russia had not known since the days of Lenin. Those early days of revolutionary fervour were now consciously invoked, and figures from this heroic period of Soviet Russia's past became symbolic. Such was Yesenin, a poet of peasant origin who committed suicide in 1925, whose personal sincerity was hailed by Yevtushenko in the following lines

Who says that you were supine?
Keeping faith with truth, however quietly, needs spirit.
You were truer to the Party than those swine
who always tried to tell you how to serve it.

And keeping my honour as a citizen
in all the wrangles of our communal Parnassus,
if only for the reason that you bore Yesenin,
I rejoice: Russia, you are marvellous!

First page of the autograph of the eleventh (1905) symphony composed in 1957. The movement is entitled 'Palace Square' (Reprinted by permission of Lawrence and Wishart Ltd)

In keeping with this mood of enthusiasm for what has been called 'revolutionary romanticism' and 'the revival of Leninist norms' Shostakovich was inspired to compose a symphonic diptych commemorating the two revolutions of 1905 and 1917 — works whose public oratory contrasts sharply with the intimate musings

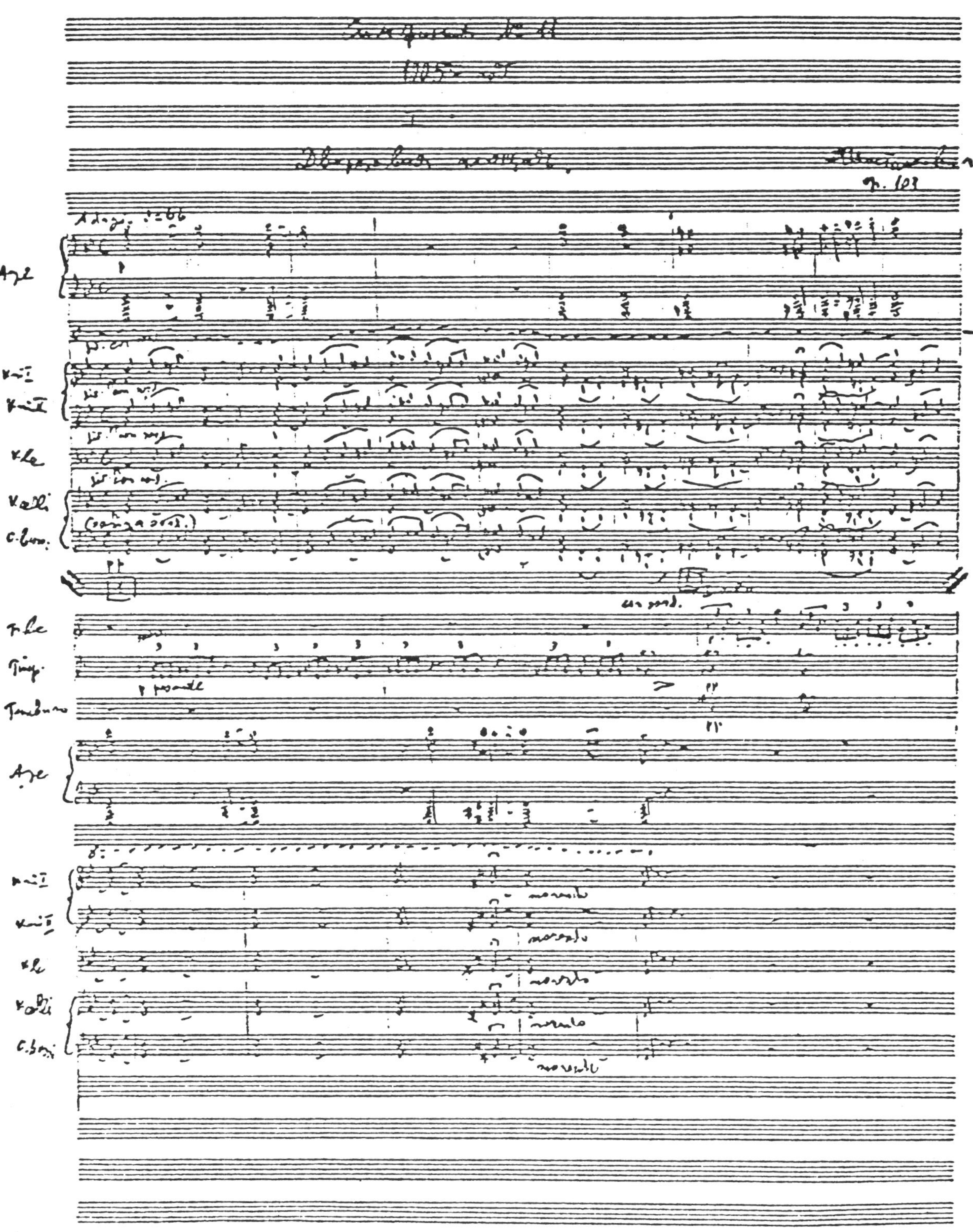

of, say, the first movement of the Violin Concerto which a now 'humanised' Russia was beginning to take to its heart, through the persuasive advocacy of David Oistrakh. The eleventh symphony was performed in Moscow on the 40th anniversary of the October Revolution and four days later heard in Leningrad, the city which had been at the centre of those distant stirring events of 1905. Its success was enormous. A distinguished politician, in Moscow for the celebrations, recalls the reception:

> The symphony was over . . . the public, the whole of the huge crowded hall and we with them, were seething with excitement. Whether he wanted to or not the composer of this magnificent revolutionary work had to go on to the stage and accept the stormy applause. But the soviet people honoured him justly as a man who had enriched their culture and the culture of mankind with an undying work of art.

The second panel of the diptych was the twelfth symphony, 'The Year 1917' which Shostakovich composed four years later in 1961 and dedicated to the memory of Lenin. To this we shall return in its proper chronological place.

1958 was the year of the Pasternak-Zhivago affair, in which the distinguished Russian author was considered in leading literary circles to have gone too far in his portrayal of private, non-political emotions and attitudes during the days of Civil War and the New Economic Policy. The novel was, for a variety of reasons, withheld from publication in Soviet Russia. Chief amongst these reasons was the uncertainty that prevailed at the time as to the permissible limits of subjectivity and personal expression. As is well known, the book was published abroad, gaining its author a Nobel Prize, and Pasternak became identified in the West as amongst the first in a growing movement of 'dissent' which followed Khrushchev's political demise. As we shall see, this mood of uncertainty as to the acceptable bounds of personal outspokenness was soon to affect Shostakovich's own, most openly dissenting work, the thirteenth symphony.

But not yet. With official recognition at home and abroad — the list of honours was such that Shostakovich made it the subject of an elaborate joking 'Preface to the complete collection of my works' on his 60th birthday — the composer was riding high on a tide of world-wide popular and official Soviet acclaim. This culminated in his being appointed First Secretary of the Russian division of the National Composers' Union, an appointment which necessitated his becoming a member of the Party in 1960.

Perhaps his most important trip abroad at this time was his visit to the U.S.A. on 22nd October 1959 as a member of a Soviet delegation of composers and critics headed by Khrennikov,

The first performance of the eleventh symphony in Moscow, 30th October 1957. USSR State Symphony Orchestra conducted by Nikolai Rachlin (Novosti)

Cultural thaw, 1960. Shostakovich is presented with a diploma making him an honorary member of the American National Institute of Arts by American composers Lukas Foss and Aaron Copland (Novosti)

Chairman of the Composers' Union. It was a more cordial event that his earlier conscripted visit in Stalinist 1949, but the composer's distaste for such political/cultural missions was noted by a reporter who described Shostakovich as 'highly nervous, a chain smoker with darting eyes and fidgeting hands, ill at ease most of the time'.

The visit was important for the launching of a new work. Shostakovich brought with him his first cello concerto composed for Rostropovich, fresh from its first performance in Moscow on October 9th. After its first American performance in Philadelphia Edwin H. Schloss reported in *The Philadelphia Inquirer*

The music is in a technical sense admirably written for the instrument, thanks no doubt to the fact that the score was written for and dedicated to Rostropovich. And on Friday the dedicatee gave it a magnificent performance on the Academy stage. Rostropovich is a gallant master of his instrument. His technical equipment is nothing less than astounding. In the cadenza he employed every trick of the trade with consummate facility. His cantabile tone was full and round — a sine qua non of fine cello playing — and his taste and musicianship were in evidence all the time. On the pyrotechnic side he threw in runs and double stops in the most difficult 'thumb' positions: stopped and natural harmonics in dazzling and left hand pizzicato profusion, dashed off with an élan that was irresistible.

Another highly subjective autobiographical work appeared the following year — the eighth quartet, 'dedicated to the memory of the victims of Fascism and war'. In Shostakovich's words

Khrushchev addresses a conference of agricultural workers in 1961 (SCR)

It happened like this — I went to Dresden where our Mosfilm group happened to be at the time, making a film called 'The Five Days and Nights' about the rescuing of the treasures in the Dresden Gallery. And Dresden made a terrific impact on me, the frightful and senseless destruction; because Dresden had been savagely bombed when it was quite obvious who was going to win the war. And this devastated city reminded me of our own devastated cities that I'd been in, and of the human victims, the many lives taken away by the war that Hitler's fascism unleashed. All this made such a profound impression on me that in three days I had the quartet completely finished.

At the centre of this composition the composer's 'I' — DSCH pervades this work as never before in a composition by Shostakovich, to an obsessive degree. The quartet is rich in self quotations.

The following year, 1961, witnessed the première of two very different works: the one public and patriotic, the other much the reverse. On 15th October Moscow audiences received the twelfth symphony, subtitled 'The Year 1917' and dedicated to the memory of Lenin. Although a stirring and profoundly organic work, its manifest programmatic content aroused less enthusiasm than its predecessor. Abroad, it came to be under-estimated. It was, in any case, overshadowed by the first performance on 30th December in Moscow under Kondrashin of the long withheld fourth symphony. 'Let them eat it' Shostakovich is reported to have said as he sat through Kondrashin's rehearsal of this staggering unheard masterpiece, 25 years old. The English critic Robert Henderson was present at the 1962 Western première in Edinburgh. He wrote

By chance I found myself sitting in the row immediately behind the composer and a few seats away on the curve to his right. Though elsewhere, in the foyers and Press conferences, he had created an impression of extreme diffidence and nervousness, he betrayed throughout the symphony itself no perceptible reaction, retaining a kind of stoical calm which to the casual observer seemed strangely to contradict the music's almost neurasthenic, wildly turbulent nature.

The violence and tragedy of this work spoke prophetically for its time, and at this première English audiences were able to identify with a historic document which seemed to speak not only of the horrors of Stalin's Russia in the 1930's but for the fears of a whole generation in Europe who knew of the suffering of those in Hitler's concentration camps and feared the end of civilisation in a Second World War. The relevance of this overwhelming piece to what had been going on in Stalin's Russia was further re-inforced by the publication (said to be authorised by Khrushchev himself) in the following year of Solzhenitsyn's *One day in the life of Ivan*

The title page of the first printed edition of the fourth symphony, Op.43, published in 1962. The symphony was first performed on December 30th 1961, twenty-five years after its completion.

Д. ШОСТАКОВИЧ
D. SHOSTAKOVICH

ор. 43

СИМФОНИЯ №4
SYMPHONY №4

ПАРТИТУРА
SCHORE

«СОВЕТСКИЙ КОМПОЗИТОР»
«SOVIET COMPOSER»
Москва 1962 Moscow

Denisovich. This description of life in a Siberian labour camp was greeted as 'a blow struck for human freedom all over the world'.

But the most dramatic event of all during this seemingly endless succession of exciting Shostakovich premières was still to come — the première on 18th December 1962 of the thirteenth symphony for bass soloists, chorus and orchestra to texts selected by the composer from Yevtushenko. Boris Schwarz, who was in Moscow at the time, tells the story:

The première of the Thirteenth Symphony was awaited in Moscow with intense anticipation. The excitement generated was not purely musical: people were aware of the artistic tensions behind the scene, of the meetings between the arts intelligentsia and the Party. The city was buzzing with rumour of a possible last-minute cancellation of the performance. The dress rehearsal was open to conservatory students and faculty members. A staff member of the Glinka Museum emerged from the dress rehearsal; my question about the music was waved aside, . . . 'but the WORDS'.

The words were indeed gunpowder. Not that Yevtushenko's individual poems had met with official disapproval (they had all been published), but the composer's choice for his five movements — 'Babyi Yar', 'Humour', 'In the Store', 'Fears', 'Career' — laid bare in a particularly stark way the humanist message of his symphony. Condemnation of anti-Semitism, praise of humour and non-conformity, expression of the sufferings and fears of ordinary men and women in a police state, and hope for better times, praise for great men of the past such as Galileo and Tolstoy who in their careers had not been afraid to speak the truth — this was stirring stuff, but to the authorities, inflammatory.

Boris Schwarz continues:

At the première, the government box remained unoccupied, and a planned television transmission did not take place. A listener approaching the Conservatory Hall on the evening of 18 December found the entire square cordoned off by police. Inside, the hall was filled to overflowing. The first half, consisting of Mozart's 'Jupiter' Symphony, received a minimum of attention; no one cared . . . The intermission seemed endless; finally, the chorus filed on stage, followed by the orchestra, the soloist, the conductor Kyril Kondrashin. The tension was unbearable. The first movement, *Babyi Yar,* was greeted with a burst of spontaneous applause. At the end of the hour-long work, there was an ovation rarely witnessed. On the stage was Shostakovich, shy and awkward, bowing stiffly. He was joined by Yevtushenko, moving with the ease of a born actor. Two great artists — a generation apart — fighting for the same cause — freedom of the human spirit. Seeing the pair together, the audience went wild; the rhythmic clapping, so characteristic of Russian enthusiasm, redoubled in intensity, the cadenced shouts 'Bra-vo Shos-ta-ko-vich' and 'Bra-vo- Yev-tu-shen-ko' filled the air. The audience seemed to be carried away as much by the music as by the words, although (contrary to custom) the texts were not printed in the programme distributed to the public.

The following morning, a one-sentence report appeared in *Pravda*, an absurd anti-climax for anyone who had witnessed the exciting evening.

In short, the symphony was tacitly banned — a situation to which Shostakovich was, by this time, getting accustomed. In this case, however, it was the work rather than the much honoured composer, that was to be shunned.

Hard on the heels of this performance came the first performance since 1936 of the opera *Lady Macbeth,* now retitled

Composer and poet acknowledging the applause after the first performance of the thirteenth symphony, Moscow 1962 (Novosti)

Title page of the first edition of the thirteenth symphony, perhaps the composers most openly 'dissident' work, and not published until 1971 — nine years after its first performance

Д. ШОСТАКОВИЧ
D. SHOSTAKOVICH
Op. 113

ТРИНАДЦАТАЯ СИМФОНИЯ

THIRTEENTH SYMPHONY

ДЛЯ СОЛИСТА БАСА, ХОРА БАСОВ И СИМФОНИЧЕСКОГО ОРКЕСТРА

FOR BASS SOLO, BASS CHORUS AND SYMPHONY ORCHESTRA

Слова Е. ЕВТУШЕНКО
Words by Ye. YEVTUSHENKO

ПАРТИТУРА
SCORE

СОВЕТСКИЙ КОМПОЗИТОР
SOVIET COMPOSER
Москва 1971 Moscow

Katerina Ismailova. This took place at the Stanislavsky-Nemirovich-Danchenko Theatre in Moscow on 8th January under conditions of minimum publicity and, indeed, amusing duplicity. The plan was to schedule a performance of Rossini's *Barber of Seville* and at the last minute to 'substitute' Shostakovich's opera. The ruse worked. For those in the know 'See you at the Barber' had the significance of a wink and nobody wished to change their ticket when they heard that there had been

Stravinsky arrives in Soviet Russia, September 1962 — his first visit to the country for forty-eight years. Khrennikov in the foreground (Novosti)

a 'change of programme'. Boris Schwarz, who attended the performance, reports:

It was a blazing performance, perhaps not fully polished as yet, but sung with passion by a youthful cast, in the actor-singer tradition of the founders of the theatre. The staging and direction were ingenious, avoiding extreme naturalism, yet conveying all the raw passions of the libretto. The amusing scene in the police station (unfortunately omitted at the New York revival in 1965) served as an ironic reminder that, after all, police methods had not changed very much.

— 'Begin, murderer!' Scene from the film 'Hamlet' directed by G. Kozintsev with music by Shostakovich, July 1963. "I'm particularly touched by Hamlet's conversation with Rosenkrantz and Guildenstern, when Hamlet says that he's not a pipe and won't let people play him." A revealing comment on the play by Shostakovich in conversation with Volkov. (Novosti)

Time and again, all eyes in the audience turned to the composer who sat in the centre of the stalls; he seemed oblivious to the surroundings as he listened — fully absorbed — to the savage realism and impassioned surge of his youthful score. The ovation at the end was more than a tribute to a great composer; it seemed that every listener identified himself with this historic act of vindication. Shostakovich appeared on the stage in the midst of the applauding performers. His sensitive face was haggard and showed the emotional strain. He had won a battle — but at what price!

The return of Stravinsky to his native Russia after fifty years of self imposed exile had been another symbol of cultural thaw in 1962. Shostakovich, who had a great admiration for certain of Stravinsky's works (an admiration which, it must be admitted, was not reciprocated by Stravinsky) explained to Volkov that

'The invitation . . . was the result of high politics. At the very top it was decided to make him the Number One national composer, but this gambit didn't work. Stravinsky hadn't forgotten anything — that he had been called a lackey of American imperialism and a flunkey of the Catholic Church — and the very same people who had called him that were now greeting him with outspread arms.'

Shostakovich and Stravinsky found themselves together at a number of more or less official occasions during the visit. At a

Britten and Shostakovich in London, 1964 (Novosti)

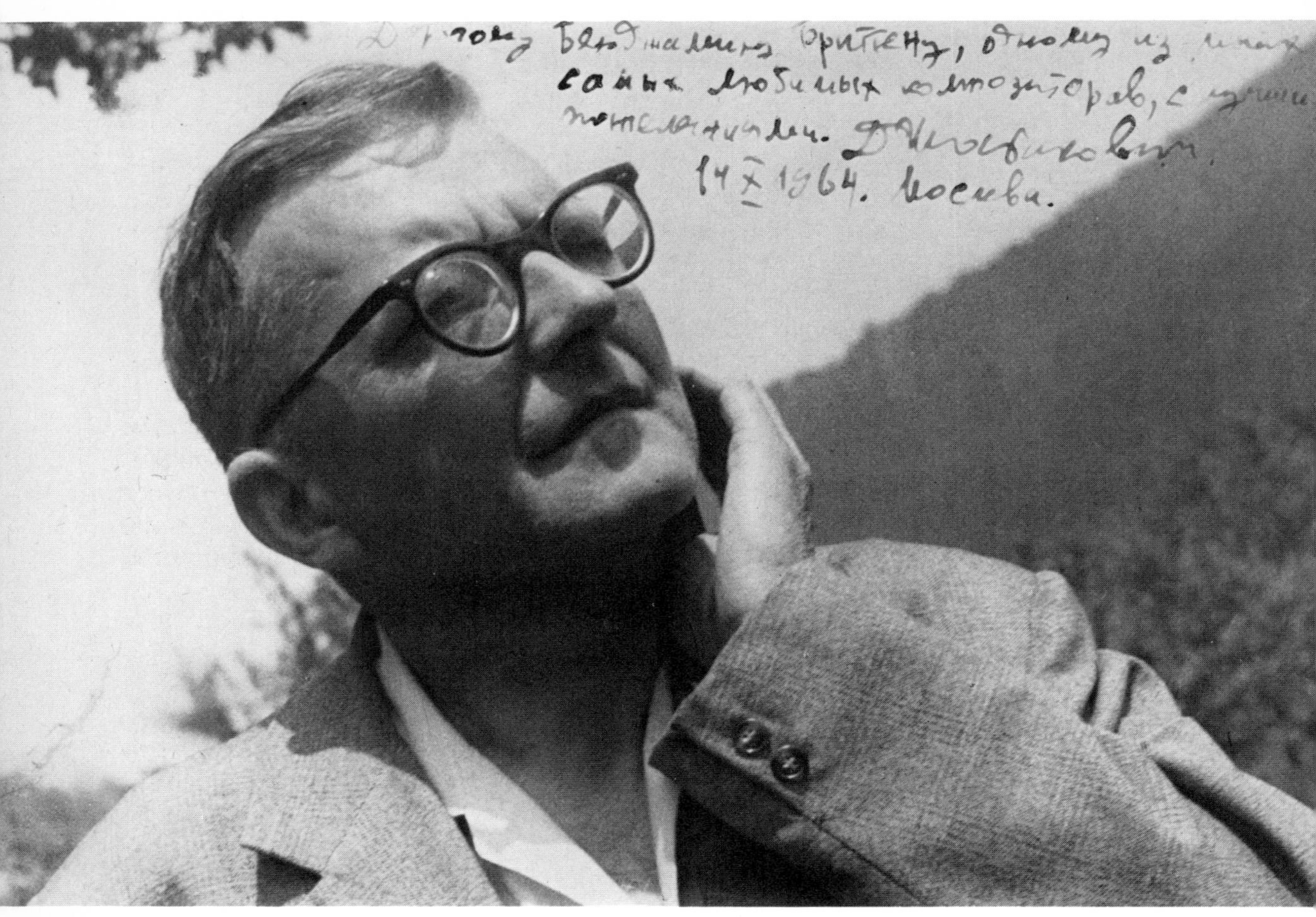

Autographed photograph for Benjamin Britten. The inscription reads: 'To dear Benjamin Britten, one of my most beloved composers. With best wishes. D. Shostakovich 14.X.1964. Moscow' (Britten Estate)

reception given by the Minister of Culture on October 1st the conductor and diarist Robert Craft described the composer:

Shostakovich's is the most 'sensitive' and intellectual face we have so far seen in the USSR. He is thinner, taller, younger — more boyish looking — than expected, but he is also the shyest and most nervous human being I have ever seen. He chews not merely his nails but his fingers, twitches his pouty mouth and chin, chain-smokes, wiggles his nose in constant adjustment of his spectacles, looks querulous one moment and ready to cry the next. His hands tremble, he stutters, his whole frame wobbles when he shakes hands — which reminds us of Auden — and his knees knock when he speaks, at which time the others look anxious for him, as indeed they might. He has a habit of staring, too, then of turning guiltily away when caught, and all evening long he peeks illicitly at I.S. around the nicely rounded corners of Mme Furtseva. There is no betrayal of the thoughts behind those frightened, very intelligent eyes. His new wife sits beside him. An adoring pupil, perhaps, but by age, looks, and her equally shy, serious, distant manner, a daughter . . .

In March 1963 Shostakovich made the personal acquaintance of another composer for whom he already entertained a great admiration: the forty-nine year old Benjamin Britten from Aldeburgh, England. In this case the admiration was mutual. Ever since attending a pre-war performance of Shostakovich's *Lady Macbeth* Britten had entertained a high regard for his Soviet colleague, and this visit, during a Festival of British Music from 6th–19th March, initiated a warm artistic friendship that ceased only with Shostakovich's death thirteen years later. Britten's personality and music appealed strongly to colleagues and audiences alike in the Soviet Russia of the time, and the Festival proved the first of several creatively fruitful trips which revolved round the cellist Rostropovich as chief host. (Britten and Pears cordially returned this hospitality at Aldeburgh where several of Shostakovich's works were heard, including the first performance outside Russia of the fourteenth symphony in 1970.) To one of Britten's holidays in Russia we owe Peter Pears' account of a Christmas visit to Shostakovich's dacha outside Moscow on Saturday, 31st December 1966.

We were summoned for 10 p.m. at Dmitri's, we were of course late. The surprise was a special showing of an ancient copy of *The Gold Rush* upstairs in someone's bedroom. (It is the most wonderful film and full of superb sophisticated photography — don't forget the Chaplin-into-Hen sequence). We had a quick nip of vodka before, and the film lasted exactly the right length of time (until 11.50) when with champagne bottles in hand we went out to the brightly lit Christmas Tree and toasted the New Year to the Soviet National Anthem, and went round kissing one another, the Shostakoviches, the Professor and his family, Dmitri's daughter Galya and her very odd beatnik husband, and us. Next came a meal round a long table groaning with drink and eats, and presents (indoors, needless to say). We each got some cognac or vodka, a false nose (not expected to be worn for more than a minute or two) and, later, a score of Dmitri's recent *Stepan Razin* (Yevtushenko) for Ben, and a record of same for me. At this point Dmitri, tired, and with a recent heart attack in mind, was packed off to bed,

The heart attack to which Sir Peter referred had come shortly after a 60th birthday concert in May that year in which the composer had partnered the bass, Yevgeni Nesterenko, at the piano in the first performances of two new works. One of these was the afore-mentioned ironic *Preface to the Complete Collection of my Works and Brief Reflections apropos this Preface*. The mocking self irony of this piece reveals itself in an intoned list of the composer's 'honorific titles, extremely responsible duties and assignments' and the motto DSCH. And, indeed, both the eleventh string quartet and the second cello concerto (performed on his 60th

At the Grand Concert given in Moscow on the occasion of Shostakovich's 60th birthday, 25th September, 1966. The composer takes his share of the applause with the soloist after the first performance of the second cello concerto by its dedicatee, Mstislav Rostropovich. 'When thunderous applause draws him onto the stage, he clutches nervously for the hand of the conductor' (in this case, the soloist) 'jerkily takes his bow to the audience and hurries from the hall'. Martynov. (Novosti)

birthday in Moscow by Rostropovich) seem to bring this same wry element of painful self irony to the fore. In particular the second cello concerto strikes a new, grimmer, even macabre note in Shostakovich. The energy is undiminished, but in the dark prelude, the manic scherzo and the ambiguously turned finale (with its mocking return of the scherzo at the climax) we sense the autobiography of a composer who has become aware of his personal mortality for the first time. This dark work has, indeed, something of the same terror and sense of life's transient beauty that may be experienced in Schoenberg's String Trio, written after its composer had experienced a similar physical trauma. These works inaugurated Shostakovich's final period of creative development.

Chapter 13

Works of Last Period and Death (1966–1975)

'The owl of Minerva takes her flight at dusk'

Hegel

In his last years the ailing composer was the subject of press, radio and TV interviews both at home and abroad, film documentaries, revivals of works long 'buried in silence' (such as the third symphony, the unfinished opera *The Gamblers* and — perhaps most sensational of all — *The Nose*) all of which suggests an almost

A still from the film of 'Katarina Ismailova' (Shostakovich's new version of *Lady Macbeth of the Mtensk District*) with Galina Vishnevskaya, wife of Rostropovich, in the title role (Novosti)

overwhelming concern to pay tribute and make amends while there was still time. In his native country he was smothered in further honours: on his sixtieth birthday a Kremlin decree conferred upon him the Order of Lenin, the title of 'Hero of Socialist Labour' and the 'Gold Hammer and Sickle Medal'. Abroad, the whole of Europe and America seemed to be vieing with each other in recognising his universal genius. Great Britain, Austria, Bavaria, Finland, Denmark, the USA, each in their turn extended invitations, and the composer continued to make short trips abroad as a recipient of these honours right up to 1973, only two years before his death, when he was in America to receive the Honorary Doctorate of Fine Arts at North Western University, Evanston, USA.

Upon the political demise of Khrushchev in 1964 the cultural climate of the thaw continued for a time. Under the new collective leadership of Kosygin and Brezhnev there were indications that young, experimentally minded artists were to be encouraged — within limits. As Secretary of the Union of Composers Shostakovich, in his public speeches and pronouncements, dutifully reflected the ever changing nuances of cultural policy. While in 1965 he was able to offer cautious encouragement to a young avant garde composer, Edison Denisov, his last speech as retiring first Secretary of the Russian Composers Union in 1968 suggested a less flexible attitude:

> The decisions of the April plenary sessions of the Party's Central Committee have made it incumbent on us to take an active stand against attempts to smuggle into individual works of literature and art views alien to the Socialist ideology of Soviet society.
>
> In this connection, I should like to touch upon the question of so-called 'avant-gardism' in music (the term . . . usurped by a small group of musicians occupying a definite position in Western art). At the base of this militant trend lies a destructive principle in relation to music . . .
>
> 'Avant-gardism' is a deliberate attempt . . . to achieve a new quality in music merely through the repudiation of historically evolved norms and rules. This is a gross theoretical error . . .
>
> We Soviet artists resolutely reject 'avant-gardism'.

But perhaps Shostakovich — who had himself 'repudiated historically evolved norms and rules' as a young man — was still something of an avant gardist at heart. Like his admired English friend and colleague, Benjamin Britten, he was able to adapt new trends such as 'serial technique' to suit his own expressive purposes. Schoenberg's method of composing with twelve notes related only to one another (resulting in his systematic use of a single 'row' of twelve notes as the basis of an entire composition) had become fashionable in the West. In his monumental twelfth String Quartet of 1968 Shostakovich had himself adapted Schoenberg's technique, producing a level of dissonance which must have made Zhdanov writhe in his grave, but he was careful that the dissonances eventually resolved. The music remained basically simple, singable and firmly rooted in a key centre, true to Shostakovich's ideal of 'accessibility'. It was as if there had been no Schoenberg 'crisis' in music, despite his utilisation of Schoenberg's techniques. With this recent creative experience in mind the composer was able to say in an interview for the publication *Youth* in 1968:

> . . . everything is good in moderation . . . The use of elements from these complex systems is entirely justified if it is dictated by the idea of the composition . . . Please understand that the formula 'the end justifies the means' to some extent seems right to me in music. Any means? Any, as long as they convey the goal.

The twelfth quartet, first performed in Leningrad on 14th September 1968 by the Beethoven Quartet, was Shostakovich's last attempt at an optimistic finale — something which had never come easily to him but had so often been expected of him. In it he deliberately invokes the Beethovenian 'world of high ideals' in conflict with 'the agonising impossibility of solving the contradictions of life'.* In short, the quartet wins through to heroic affirmation after a life and death struggle with the powers of darkness. Perhaps, though, that heroic affirmation is an effort of will rather than a genuine conviction that 'all will be well'.

It is difficult to discuss the last years of Shostakovich's life except in terms of his music. Unconsciously, the idea had come to him of writing a set of late quartets as a kind of spiritual last will and testament in the tradition of his great idol, Beethoven. And in these quartets we enter a unique world of personal isolation and despair in the contemplation of death. If the experience is at times harrowing we must remember that physical infirmity was making life a burden to him — a burden which, however, never impaired a razor-sharp mind and a vigorous composing technique.

The sadness and isolation of these years are vividly caught in a sequence from a Soviet documentary film made in 1971. As a Moscow journalist put it:

> . . . The composer is seated in the compartment of a speeding train, looking into the window mournfully streaked with rain . . . No glimmer of satisfaction passes across the pale face with its tightly compressed lips.

Rostropovich's 'Open Letter to Pravda' (which was not printed by that paper) as it appeared in the New York Times, Monday 16th November, 1970. The Russian cellist, a close colleague of the composer and dedicatee of the two cello concertos, has lived in the West since 1974. He was deprived of his Soviet citizenship in 1978. (© 1970 by the New York Times Company. Reprinted by permission)

* Translated programme note to the first English performance, referred to by Hans Keller in his article on the Quartet in Tempo 94, Autumn 1970.

An Open Letter to Pravda

A Distinguished Soviet Artist Appeals For Solzhenitsyn

By MSTISLAV ROSTROPOVICH

Open letter

To the chief editors of the newspapers Pravda, Izvestia, Literaturnaya Gazeta, and Sovetskaya Kultura.

Esteemed Comrade Editor:

It is no longer a secrêt that A. I. Solzhenitsyn lives a great part of the time in my house near Moscow. I have seen how he was expelled from the Writers' Union—at the very time when he was working strenuously on a novel about the year 1914. Now the Nobel Prize has been awarded to him. The newspaper campaign in this connection compels me to undertake this letter to you.

In my memory this is already the third time that a Soviet writer has been given the Nobel Prize. In two cases out of three we have considered the awarding of the prize a "dirty political game," but in one (Sholokhov) as a "just recognition" of the outstanding world significance of our literature.

If in his time Sholokhov had declined to accept the prize from hands which had given it to Pasternak "for Cold War considerations" I would have understood that we no longer trusted the objectivity and the honesty of the Swedish academicians. But now it happens that we selectively sometimes accept the Nobel Prize with gratitude and sometimes curse it.

And what if next time the prize is awarded to Comrade Kochetov [Vsevolod Kochetov, Soviet author and hard line editor]? Of course it will have to be accepted!

Why, a day after the award of the prize to Solzhenitsyn, in our papers appeared a strange report of correspondent "X" with representatives of the secretariat of the Writers' Union to the effect that the entire public of the country (that is evidently all scholars and all musicians, etc.) actively supported his expulsion from the Writers' Union?

Why does Literaturnaya Gazeta select from numerous Western newspapers only the opinion of American and Swedish newspapers, avoiding the incomparably more popular and important Communist newspapers like L' Humanité, Lettre Française and L'Unità, to say nothing of the numerous non-Communist ones?

If we trust a certain critic Bonosky [Philip Bonosky, an American Communist journalist], then how should we consider the opinion of such important writers as Boll, Aragon and François Mauriac

I remember and would like to remind you of our newspapers in 1948, how much nonsense was written about those giants of our music, S. S. Prokofiev and D. D. Shostakovich, who are now honored.

For example:

"Comrades D. Shostakovich, S. Prokofiev, V. Shebalin, N. Myaskovsky and others—your atonal disharmonic music is organically alien to the people ... formalistic trickery arises when there is an obvious lack of talent, but very much pretension to innovation ... we absolutely do not accept the music of Shostakovich, Myaskovsky, Prokofiev. There is no harmony in it, no order, no wide melodiousness, no melody."

Now, when one looks at the newspapers of those years, one becomes unbearably ashamed of many things. For the fact is that for three decades the opera, "Katerina Izmailova" [of Shostakovich] was not performed, that S. Prokoviev during his life did not hear the last version of his opera, "War and Peace," and his Symphonic Concerto for cello and orchestra, that there were official lists of forbidden works of Shostakovich, Prokofiev, Myaskovsky and Khachaturian.

Has time really not taught us to approach cautiously the crushing of talented people? And not to speak in the name of all the people? Not to oblige people to express as their opinions what they simply have not read or heard? I recall with pride that I did not go to the meeting of cultural figures in the Central House of Cultural Workers where B. Pasternak was abused and where I was expected to deliver a speech which I had been "commissioned" to deliver, criticizing "Doctor Zhivago," which at that time I had not read.

> *"Why in our literature and art so often people absolutely incompetent in this field have the final word? Why are they given the right to discredit our art in the eyes of our people?"*

In 1948 there were lists of forbidden works. Now oral prohibitions are preferred, referring to the fact that "opinions exist" that the work is not recommended. It is impossible to establish where this opinion exists and whose it is. Why for instance was Galina Vishnevskaya [Mr. Rostropovich's wife] forbidden to perform in her concert in Moscow, the brilliant vocal cycle of Boris Tchaikovsky with the words of I. Brodsky [a dissident Leningrad poet]? Why was the performance of the Shostakovich cycle to the words of Sasha Chyorny obstructed several times (although the text had already been published)? Why did difficulties accompany the performance of Shostakovich's 13th and 14th Symphonies?

Again, apparently, "there was an opinion." Who first had the "opinion" that it was necessary to expel Solzhenitsyn from the Writers' Union? I did not manage to clarify this question although I was very interested in it. Did five Ryazan writer-musketeers really dare to do it themselves without a serious "opinion"?

Apparently the "opinion" prevented also my fellow citizens from getting to know Tarkovsky's film "Andrey Rublyov," which we sold abroad and which I had the pleasure of seeing among enraptured Parisians. Obviously it was "opinion" which also prevented publication of Solzhenitsyn's "Cancer Ward," which was already set in type for Novy Mir [the leading Soviet literary journal]. So if this had been published here it would have been openly and widely discussed to the benefit of the author as well as the readers.

I do not speak about political or economic questions in our country. There are people who know these better than I. But explain to me please, why in our literature and art so often people absolutely incompetent in this field have the final word? Why are they given the right to discredit our art in the eyes of our people?

I recall the past not in order to grumble but in order that in the future, let's say in 20 years, we won't have to bury today's newspapers in shame.

Every man must have the right fearlessly to think independently and express his opinion about what he knows, what he has personally thought about, experienced and not merely to express with slightly different variations the opinion which has been inculcated in him.

We will definitely arrive at reconstruction without prompting and without being corrected.

I know that after my letter there will undoubtedly be an "*opinion*" about me, but I am not afraid of it. I openly say what I think. Talent, of which we are proud, must not be submitted to the assaults of the past. I know many of the works of Solzhenitsyn. I like them. I consider he seeks the right through his suffering to write the truth as he saw it and I see no reason to hide my attitude toward him at a time when a campaign is being launched against him.

Moscow, 31 October, 1970.

Mstislav Rostropovich, the world-famous cellist, addressed the above letter to the Soviet press, which has not published it.

The fingers of his nervous hands are never at rest. And in the eyes from beneath the heavily rimmed glasses can be caught flashes of anger, pain and courage. Such is the face of the musician who is called the 'musical conscience of the century'. The moment reproduced on the screen is extremely meaningful. For those who have come into contact with Shostakovich, it is his life. They know his inscrutable face with its strange tremor. They know his passion for confession in music, which may overtake him in any surroundings . . .

Musical friendships, however, remained — and there were new ones to come. There was Rostropovich — soon to find himself a permanent exile for his outspokenness on behalf of Solzhenitsyn; there was Britten, with whom Rostropovich had already struck up a close and stimulating musical rapport; there was his son, Maxim, who was now dedicating his talents as a rising young conductor to the performance of his father's works. The new friendship, coming at the very end of the composer's life, was with a young English quartet which wrote for permission to perform the thirteenth quartet. To this we shall shortly return.

Meanwhile the composer's association with Britten led him in 1969 to dedicate a new symphony for two singers, strings and percussion, the fourteenth to his friend. The idea for the fourteenth symphony — a cycle of songs to poems about death by various poets — had come to him some time previously, when, in 1962, he had been working on an orchestration of Mussorgsky's *Songs and Dances of Death*. Shostakovich's creative friendship with Britten is touchingly expressed in his setting of the poem *O Delvig, Delvig* not only in the musical imagery (which echoes Britten's own simple, direct style) but in the words of the poem itself that, as from one poet to another, speaks of immortality and the beauty of art and friendship. The line about 'villains and fools' suggests, inevitably, the abuse which the great Russian composer had had to endure in Soviet Russia.

O Delvig, Delvig! What reward
for lofty deeds and poetry?
For talent what comfort
among villains and fools? . . .
Immortality is equally the lot
of bold, inspired deeds
and sweet songs!
Thus will not die our bond,
free, joyful and proud.
In happiness and in sorrow it stands firm,
the bond of eternal lovers of the Muses.

This is the heart of the song cycle. Its gentle philosophic musing — with Shostakovich's typical sharp sense of contrast — is

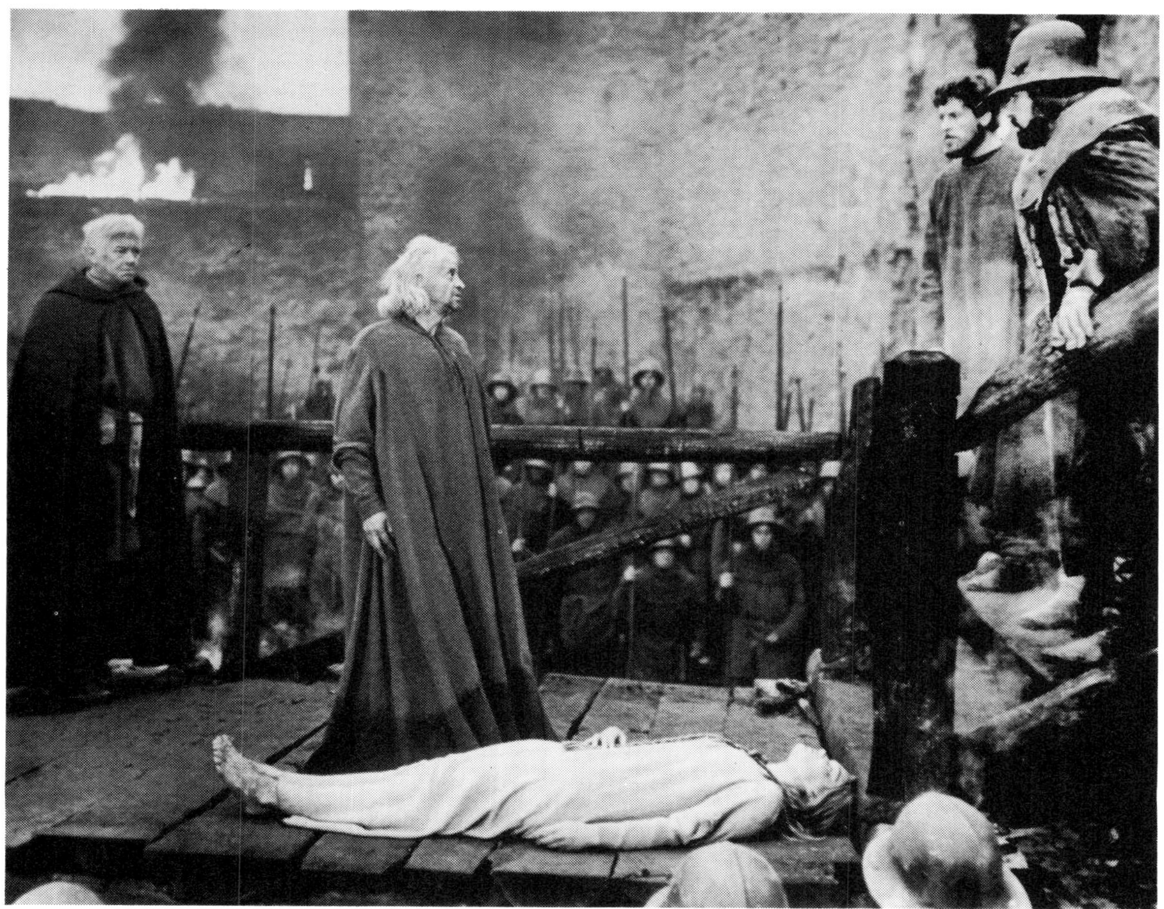

The death of Cordelia. A scene from the film of Shakespeare's 'King Lear' (directed by G. Kozintsev) to which Shostakovich wrote the music in 1970 (Novosti)

preceded by the fierce contempt of Apollinaire's *Zaporozhye Cossacks Reply to the Sultan of Constantinople*. This setting was not — as is sometimes supposed — directly inspired by Repin's famous painting, regarded throughout Russia as a national icon. The inspiration came, as it were, through refraction, since that painting was the source of the poet's stimulus, not the composer's.

Writing shortly after the first performance of the work in the UK given at Aldeburgh on 14th June 1970 under Benjamin Britten himself, the critic Peter Heyworth described the score as

> an exploration of an intensely personal, interior world on a scale that Shostakovich has reserved for his more public utterances.

As a pendant to this work, and making much use of its imagery, Shostakovich composed in 1970 the thirteenth String Quartet, perhaps the darkest and most intense of the four quartets (Nos. 11, 12, 13 and 14) each dedicated to an individual member of the Beethoven Quartet. This work, which received its Leningrad première on 13th September, was dedicated to the original viola player Vadim Borissovsky who was already mortally ill and who had had to be replaced. There is no need of words to convey the grim, desolate message of this quartet — and yet the fierce energy and unified contrast of moods in this piece show, paradoxically, an undiminished vitality and, indeed, a boldness of style that comes close to 'avant gardism'. It was this same thirteenth quartet that in 1972 brought about a touching friendship between the Fitzwilliam Quartet and the stricken composer which continued until the time of his death three years later. The viola player, Alan George, recollects:

Early that year I wrote to Shostakovich requesting his permission to perform the thirteenth quartet — the work had in fact been composed two years previously, and it seemed shameful to me that it had not yet been heard in this country. He replied at once, not only consenting but welcoming the chance and expressing the hope that he might be able to come and hear the performance himself. Not long after he sent a score and a set of parts, repeating his wish to come and hear us play. At the time I was somewhat perplexed as to why he should be so enthusiastic about hearing a very young and unknown group play his music but as I got to know him better, through his letters, his music, and meeting him personally, I have come to realise that, distressingly conscious of his age, he must have felt glad to know that this old-man's-music could live and

Shostakovich with members of the Fitzwilliam Quartet, York 1972 (Reprinted by permission of York and County Press (Westminster Press Ltd))

thrive in the hands of young people. When I received notification of the time of his arrival in York I knew that he had been unfailing in his promise to us — the first of a number of occasions on which he was equally faithful to his word. I also think that, despite his incredible modesty, he was aware of how much it meant to us — or to any musician — to have the opportunity to play to him.

I had been delegated by my colleagues to meet the composer at the station, and as I stood waiting excitement and apprehension in turn prevented me from realising the composure with which I had hoped to greet him. Of course I recognised him instantly, but he was a much bigger man than I had expected; in fact he appeared a squarely-built, powerful-looking figure, yet physically very frail on account of his poor health. His face was white and drawn, yet behind a pair of very thick spectacles one was acutely conscious of his dark, searching eyes. His reputation for being excessively nervous was soon amply justified, especially when confronted with anything more than the smallest group of people, but as he got to know us better he became more relaxed and very talkative. He must have known that actually playing to him for the first time would be a real ordeal for us, so he suggested that we should play the piece through to him during the afternoon, so that we would feel more at ease in the concert itself. At the end he seemed satisfied, and confined his remarks to amending a few of his own dynamic marks (particularly for *pizzicato*) in the text. We were all deeply touched by his efforts to make us comfortable and his insistence that plans for the day should be arranged to suit our convenience rather than his.

I don't think that anyone who was fortunate enough to be in the Lyons Concert Hall at York University that night can have forgotten the occasion very quickly. The man's presence was electrifying, and one had the overwhelming sensation that one was in the company of something indescribably great.

Although Shostakovich — as his interviews abroad testify — could sound breathlessly talkative, the words pouring out in a jabbing, nervous torrent, the cellist, Rostropovich, portrays a different side of the man, when he was unable to talk at all:

He just wanted to have the presence of a person he liked, sitting without a word in the same room. Before we lived in the same apartment building (The Composers' House in Moscow) he lived quite a long way away. He would telephone me and say 'Come quickly, hurry'.

So I'd arrive at his flat and he'd say 'Sit down, and now we can be silent.' I would sit for half an hour, without a word. It was most relaxing, just sitting. Then Shostakovich would get up and say 'Thank you. Goodbye Slava'.

It must be remembered that the Russian tongue was a great stimulus to Shostakovich the composer and it is chiefly the formidable language barrier that prevents audiences in the West from getting to know the many song cycles he composed. (Amongst his last works were a big song cycle, the monumental

Фитцвильям Квартет
Университета города Йорка

Дорогие друзья!

Спасибо Вам за письмо со всеми радостными для меня известиями. Шлю Вам мою горячую благодарность за то, что Вы выучили и сыграли мой 14-й квартет.

Я также и с большой радостью вспоминаю нашу встречу в Йорке. Я очень надеюсь, что еще много раз буду встречаться с Вами и наслаждаться Вашим искусством.

Шлю Вам самые лучшие пожелания.

Д. Шостакович

6 IX 1974. Москва

A letter from the composer to the Fitzwilliam Quartet in 1974. It reads 'To the Fitzwilliam Quartet of the University of York.
Dear friends,
Thank you for your letter and news which gave me great pleasure. I send you my warmest thanks for mastering and performing my 14th quartet.
I often, and with great pleasure, recall the reception you gave me in York. I very much hope that I shall meet with you again many times, and enjoy and admire your art.
I send you my very best wishes.
D. Shostakovich
6 IX 1974 Moscow
(by kind permission of Alan George)

The composer with his wife at a rehearsal in Moscow, 1974 (John Goodyear)

Suite on Verses of Michelangelo, for bass and piano (later orchestrated) and the *Captain Lebjadkin Verses* — from Dostoyevsky's novel *The Possessed*.) Consequently, it is as a composer of symphonic music that he is best known to audiences in England. In this connection it is interesting to recall Shostakovich's crisp response to a question from the BBC producer, Ian Engelmann, who interviewed him in Moscow in February 1974, when working on his film *Music from the Flames*.

Engelmann Why do you prefer the symphonic form?

DS I think your question could have been better put. As you know, I've written a great many different works — I have 143 opus numbers so far — and only 15 of them are symphonies. I write music in the most varied genres.

Even so, few would dispute the overriding importance of the purely instrumental fifteenth symphony which had been given its première in Moscow on 8th January 1972 by the Soviet Radio Orchestra under the composer's son Maxim. This is an enigmatic work, rich in quotations — Rossini, Wagner, Glinka, and Shostakovich himself — which, according to Shostakovich, gripped him in its writing as never before. Work never stopped on

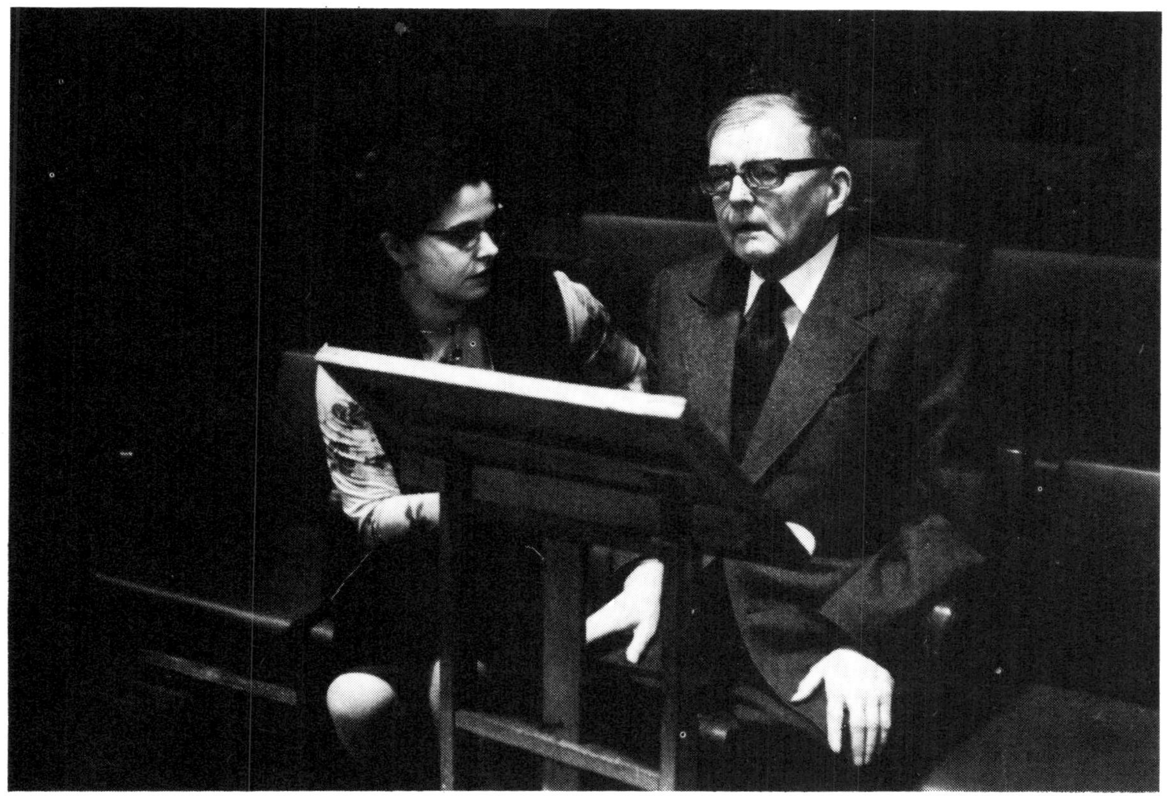

this symphony — even in hospital. Perhaps there was some deep urge to attempt a musical self portrait from childhood to the grave. The Rossini *William Tell* quotation is said to have been amongst the composer's first musical impressions. After a sad funeral march death is again to the fore in the spooky danse macabre of the scherzo, in the chilling symbolism of two '12 note' wind chords of the finale (first heard in the funeral march) which seem to stop the heart beat of this music, and the image is reinforced by frequent allusion to the well known opening phrase of Wagner's *Tristan* and the Funeral Music for *Siegfried*. Yet despite the work's maturity and nobility it still shows the composer's old capacity for self mockery and irony.

In September 1974, on his birthday there took place under the conductor Gennadi Rozhdestvensky a revival of the long unperformed *The Nose*. The intensity of this experience for the composer is movingly conveyed by the photographs of the occasion both at the first performance and during the rehearsals. For Shostakovich the work had special associations. He told Volkov

> I'm often asked why I wrote the opera *The Nose*. Well, first of all, I love Gogol. I'm not bragging, but I know pages and pages by heart. And I have striking childhood memories of *The Nose*.
>
> *The Nose* is a horror story, not a joke. How can police oppression be funny? Wherever you go, there's a policeman, you can't take a step or drop a piece of paper. And the crowd in *The Nose* isn't funny, either. Taken individually, they're not bad, just slightly eccentric. But together, they're a mob that wants blood.
>
> And there's nothing funny in the image of *The Nose*. Without a nose you're not a man, but without you the nose can become a man, and even an important bureaucrat. And there's no exaggeration here, the story is believable. If Gogol had lived in our day he would have seen stranger things. We have noses walking around such that the mind boggles, and what goes on in our republics along those lines isn't funny at all.

The composer's life was drawing to its close, but his creative energy remained undiminished to the end. That he was aware of the approaching end was clear enough — in the strange blend of quirky humour and nostalgia for vanished joys that is the fourteenth quartet, or in the spine chilling drama of the seven slow movements of the fifteenth quartet — a work which, significantly enough, bears no dedication. Art and Immortality is the pervasive theme of the lofty Verses of Michelangelo — a monumental work, dedicated to his wife, Irena. In March 1975 he completed a viola sonata in three movements, for the player of that instrument in the Beethoven Quartet, F. Druzhinin. It was to be his requiem, not performed until after his death. On Saturday, 9th August

With his son, the conductor Maxim Shostakovich, Moscow 1974 (John Goodyear)

1975, at 3.30 p.m. in the afternoon the composer died of a heart attack in the Kremlin hospital where he had been admitted ten days earlier.

The official obituary printed in the Soviet newspapers ran

In his sixty ninth year, the great composer of our times passed away — Dmitri Dmitrievich Shostakovich, Deputy of the Supreme Soviet of the USSR, laureate of the Lenin and State prizes of the USSR. A faithful son of the Communist Party, an eminent social and government figure, citizen-artist D.D.S. devoted his entire life to the development of Soviet music, reaffirming the ideals of socialist humanism and internationalism . . .

The news reached the West by the following Monday. It was rumoured that at the time of his death he was working on a sixteenth symphony with two movements completed. Perhaps — as in the case of Mahler's 10th — the world will in due course be acquainted with an as yet undisclosed chapter in the composer's autobiography. Meanwhile the fifteenth symphony and fifteenth quartet, the Michelangelo Verses and the Viola Sonata form a sufficient last will and testament.

Scene from the Moscow revival of *The Nose* in 1974 (Novosti)

The official funeral on 14th August 1975 was a solemn public occasion attended by the top cultural bureaucracy. Solomon Vokov, who was present, related

The figure who lay in the open coffin had a smile on his face. Many times I had seen him laughing, sometimes he roared with laughter. Often he had chuckled sarcastically. But I couldn't remember a smile like this: aloof and peaceful. Quiet, blissful, as though he had returned to childhood. As though he had escaped.

Outside Soviet Russia, a less public ceremony had taken place. Rostropovich heard the news of Shostakovich's death in exile while conducting at the Tanglewood Festival near Boston. Within an hour of his death his widow Irena had telephoned. Grieved by the news, Rostropovich and his wife Galina went to

a little Russian Orthodox Church near Boston. It was virtually closed, and the priest was working in a factory because there was no money for the church. We asked if a Requiem Mass could be sung for a friend. (This was because the news was not yet official). The priest recognised us and said 'Wait half an hour'. Though the total congregation was barely more than 10 on an ordinary day they managed to assemble a choir of seven. The mass was sung 'for Dimity.'

At a rehearsal of *The Nose*, revived in 1974, with the conductor Gennadi Rozhdestvensky (Novosti)

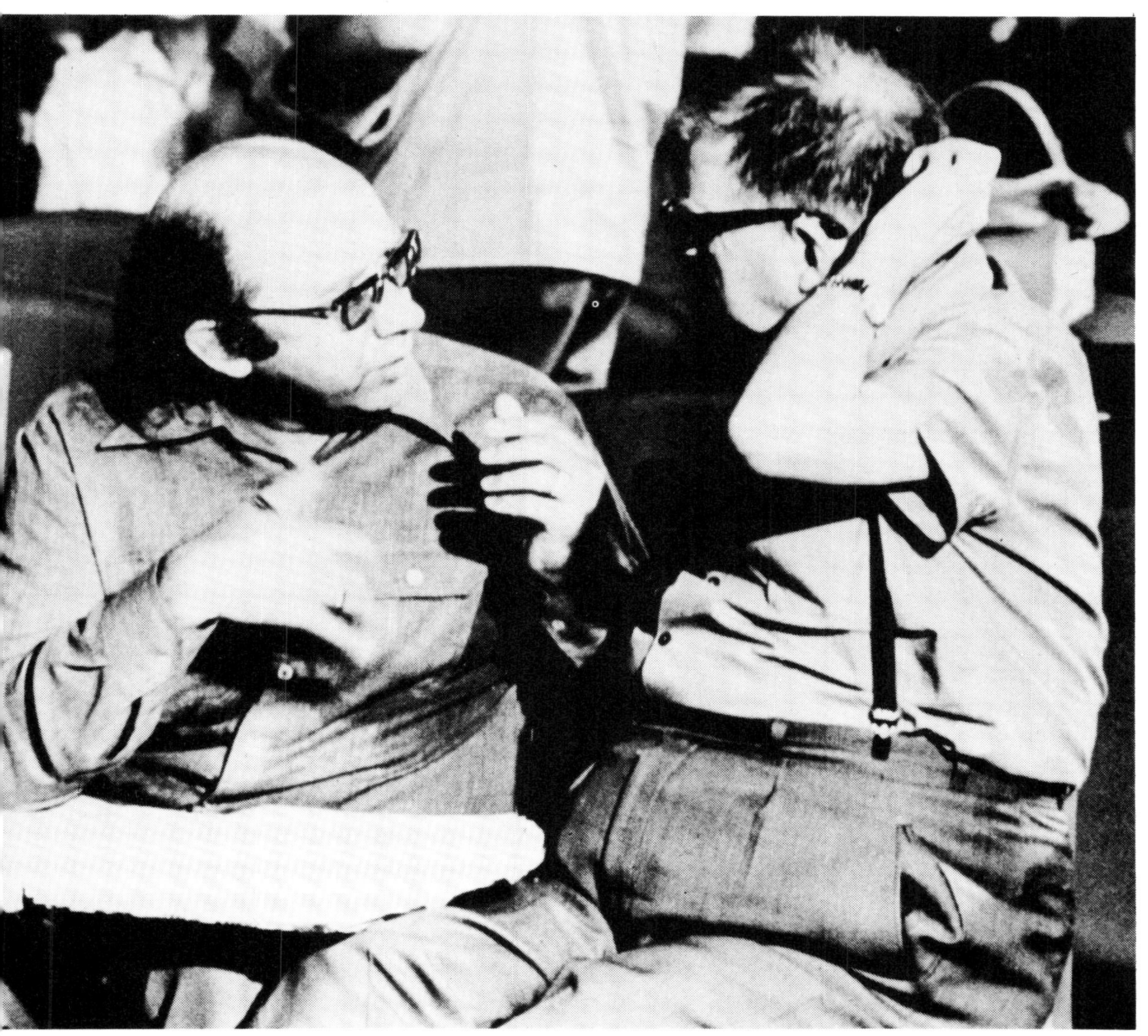

Serenade Serenade

Shostakovitch dies

By DENNIS BARKER

Dmitri Shostakovitch, the Russian composer whose work survived and paradoxically flowered in an uneasy relationship with Soviet officialdom for 50 years, has died in Moscow of a heart ailment with his sixteenth symphony only half-completed.

Shostakovich, who was 68, had had a long history of heart disease and, according to a spokesman for the Kremlin special hospital for high officials and other celebrities, had been admitted 10 days ago.

The first the West knew of his death was when the cellist Mstislav Rostropovich, a friend whose career has also experienced tremors in the embrace of officialdom, announced it to an audience in Boston, Mass. The Russian Tass news agency put out an obituary of only a few lines.

Dmitri Shostakovitch was born on September 25, 1906, in St Petersburg: a city which, as Leningrad, was later to inspire his gigantic seventh symphony, the Leningrad, performed there while it was under siege from the Germans and given its premiere in America at the same time by Toscanini.

This was in one of the periods when the composer, who was to put together over 100 works, including concertoes, operas,

Musical child of the Russian Revolution, page 11

cantatas and chamber works, and who was a defender of the Communist system, was himself in official favour.

He was not always so. He was when he wrote his first symphony at 19 as a student at Petrograd Conservatory; his fourth symphony was in 1936 described as "decadent" in one of the Stalinist pincer-movements on the arts and withdrawn before the premiere; the following year he was rehabilitated after his obeisances to "just criticism" and his universally popular fifth symphony; in 1962 his symphonic poem Babi-Yar was withdrawn because a line in it suggested continued anti-Semitism in Russia. His first opera, The Nose, a satire on power, has yet to receive official blessing.

Weathering these experiences but moving slowly into ill-health, Shostakovitch was working on his sixteenth symphony when he died.

Progress on this symphony was reported in London only last week when the Russian Ambassador, Mr Nikolai Lunkov, went to a reception given by the British recording company, EMI, who presented him with a currently produced complete album of Shostakovitch symphonies to pass on to the composer in Moscow.

Executives of EMI, now negotiating a deal for British recordings to appear in Russia, said that Shostakovitch was working slowly on his sixteenth symphony, and only two movements had been completed. His serious illness was not mentioned.

In latter years, his career had to some extent overlapped with that of his son, Maxim Shostakovitch, for whom as a pianist, it is said, Shostakovitch wrote his second piano concerto and who, as a conductor, gave wildly acclaimed performances of his father's fifth symphony. But it was his daughter Galina who yesterday confirmed at her Moscow flat that he father had died at 3.30 p.m. GMT on Saturday of a heart attack. His son, conducting in Australia, immediately cancelled his engagements.

Dmitri Shostakovitch, small, myopic, physically nervous, and the most revered Russian composer in the West, seldom gave ammunition to critics of his own country (he once accused the American conductor Leonard Bernstein of propagating a "flood of fables and nonsense" about the Soviet Union): but he was frequently vocal about official "dogmatists" in art.

It was, ironically, the man who himself died at a comparatively young age after a life of considerable illness who wrote recently in Pravda: "The desire to avoid, at any cost, everything controversial can transform young composers into young old men."

Shostakovich's obituary as it appeared in *The Guardian*, August 11th 1975. (Reprinted by permission of The Guardian)

A page from the score of the fifteenth quartet (1974) showing the 'shriek' crescendo which became a death symbol in Shostakovich's late style after the fourteenth symphony. Its origin may well lie in the famous crescendo on one note in Berg's opera *Wozzeck*, which so impressed the young Shostakovich in 1927. (Reprinted by permission of International Musikverlage Hans Sikovski)

Pravda announces the death of Shostakovich 12 August 1975 'Soviet artistic culture and progressive art of the world have suffered a heavy, irreplaceable loss. In his sixty-ninth year Dmitri Dmitrièvich shostakovich, the great composer of our times, has passed away . . .'

ПРАВДА. 12 августа 1975 г. № 224 (20828) 3

Дмитрий Дмитриевич ШОСТАКОВИЧ

Советская художественная культура, прогрессивное искусство мира понесли тяжелую, невосполнимую утрату. На 69-м году жизни скончался великий композитор нашего времени Дмитрий Дмитриевич Шостакович — депутат Верховного Совета СССР, Герой Социалистического Труда, народный артист СССР, лауреат Ленинской и Государственных премий СССР.

Верный сын Коммунистической партии, видный общественный и государственный деятель, художник - гражданин Д. Д. Шостакович всю свою жизнь посвятил развитию советской музыки, утверждению идеалов социалистического гуманизма и интернационализма, борьбе за мир и дружбу народов.

Д. Д. Шостакович родился 25 сентября 1906 года в Ленинграде. В 1925 году он окончил Ленинградскую государственную консерваторию. Уже первая симфония, которую написал девятнадцатилетний композитор, заявила о рождении могучего художественного таланта. Тема расцвета человеческой личности в революции, в нашем новом обществе определила идейно-образное содержание Пятой и Шестой симфоний, фортепианного квинтета, музыки к кинофильмам «Встречный», «Великий гражданин», к кинотрилогии о Максиме и других произведений довоенных лет. В эти же годы Д. Д. Шостакович создает оперу «Нос» по Гоголю и «Катерина Измайлова» по Лескову.

Бессмертным музыкальным памятником эпохи, волнующим художественно-политическим документом стала Седьмая симфония. Написанная в 1941 году в осажденном Ленинграде, она поведала всему миру о несгибаемой силе духа советских людей, о их вере в победу над фашизмом.

В послевоенные годы талант Д. Д. Шостаковича проявился с еще большей силой и полнотой. Композитор создал симфонии, хоровые поэмы, посвященные революции 1905 года и В. И. Ленину, которые нашли глубокий отклик в сердцах миллионов людей. Широкую известность приобрели его оратории и вокальные циклы, инструментальные концерты, квартеты и обработки народных песен, музыка ко многим кинофильмам.

Мужественно борясь с тяжелой болезнью, Д. Д. Шостакович продолжал творить вплоть до последнего дня своей жизни. Он написал произведения высочайшего философского звучания, мудрого жизнеутверждения: Пятнадцатую симфонию, Пятнадцатый квартет, где особенно ярко выступают благородство мысли композитора, его выдающееся мастерство.

Многогранное творчество Д. Д. Шостаковича — замечательный образец верности великим традициям музыкальной классики и прежде всего — русской. Он черпал вдохновение в нашей советской действительности, открывая все новые возможности ее художественного воплощения в музыке. Своим новаторским творчеством он утверждал и развивал искусство социалистического реализма, прокладывал новые пути прогрессивной мировой музыкальной культуры.

Много сил Д. Д. Шостакович отдавал общественной деятельности. Он избирался депутатом Верховного Совета СССР VI, VII, VIII, IX созывов, депутатом Верховного Совета РСФСР II, III, IV, V созывов.

В 1960—1968 гг. он возглавлял Союз композиторов РСФСР, был секретарем правления Союза композиторов СССР, членом Комитета по Ленинским и Государственным премиям при Совете Министров СССР, председателем общества «Советский Союз — Австрия». Д. Д. Шостакович избран почетным членом многих зарубежных академий и университетов.

Партия, Советское правительство высоко оценили заслуги Д. Д. Шостаковича. Ему присвоено звание народного артиста СССР, первым среди музыкантов он стал Героем Социалистического Труда. Д. Д. Шостакович награжден тремя орденами Ленина, орденами Октябрьской Революции, Трудового Красного Знамени. Ему присуждены Ленинская премия, Государственные премии СССР и РСФСР, Международная премия мира.

Человек высокого общественного долга, душевной щедрости, исключительной скромности, Д. Д. Шостакович отдал все свое творчество служению народу, Советской Родине. Он внес огромный вклад в сокровищницу отечественной и мировой художественной культуры. Гений Шостаковича, его великие творения будут жить в веках.

Л. И. Брежнев, Ю. В. Андропов, А. А. Гречко, В. В. Гришин, А. А. Громыко, А. П. Кириленко, А. Н. Косыгин, Ф. Д. Кулаков, Д. А. Кунаев, К. Т. Мазуров, А. Я. Пельше, Н. В. Подгорный, Д. С. Полянский, М. А. Суслов, В. В. Щербицкий, П. Н. Демичев, П. М. Машеров, Б. Н. Пономарев, Ш. Р. Рашидов, Г. В. Романов, М. С. Соломенцев, Д. Ф. Устинов, В. И. Долгих, И. В. Капитонов, К. Ф. Катушев, Г. Ф. Сизов, М. П. Георгадзе, А. А. Епишев, Е. М. Тяжельников, В. Ф. Шауро, С. Г. Лапин, Ф. Т. Ермаш, Б. И. Стукалин, М. Абдраев, Э. Г. Гилельс, Н. Г. Жиганов, В. Г. Загорский, Г. В. Келдыш, К. А. Караев, Д. Б. Кабалевский, Л. Б. Коган, К. П. Кондрашин, З. М. Круглова, Л. А. Кулиджанов, А. Кулиев, В. Ф. Кухарский, В. А. Лаурушас, Г. М. Марков, Ю. С. Мелентьев, Э. М. Мирзоян, Е. А. Мравинский, Г. Ш. Орджоникидзе, Г. М. Орлов, А. Н. Пахмутова, А. П. Петров, Н. А. Пономарев, Г. Г. Раман, Е. Рахмадиев, С. Т. Рихтер, Г. Н. Рождественский, А. В. Романов, Я. П. Ряэтс, П. И. Савинцев, Ш. С. Сайфиддинов, Э. Ш. Салихов, Е. Ф. Светланов, Г. В. Свиридов, В. П. Соловьев-Седой, Н. С. Тихонов, Н. В. Томский, С. С. Туликов, З. П. Туманова, К. А. Федин, А. И. Хачатурян, А. Н. Холминов, Т. Н. Хренников, М. И. Царев, Д. М. Цыганов, Б. А. Чайковский, Г. Р. Ширма, М. А. Шолохов, А. Я. Штогаренко, Р. К. Щедрин, А. Я. Эшпай, В. Н. Ягодкин.

A select bibliography of books available in English

Soviet Music and Musical Life in General

Abraham, Gerald	Eight Soviet Composers. London, 1943. OUP
Schwarz, Boris	Music and Musical Life in Soviet Russia 1917–1970. London, 1972. Barrie & Jenkins
Werth, Alexander	Musical Uproar in Moscow. London, 1949. Turnstile Press

Biographical

Malko, Nicolai	A Certain Art. New York, 1966. William Morrow & Company Inc.
Martynov, I.	Dmitri Shostakovich, the man and his work. New York, 1974. Greenwood
Rabinovich, D.	Dmitri Shostakovich. London, 1959. Lawrence & Wishart
Schwarz, Boris	Entry on Shostakovich in the new Grove, London, 1981. Macmillan Publishers
Seroff, Victor I.	Dmitri Shostakovich: the life and background of a Soviet Composer. New York, 1947. Alfred A. Knopf
Sollertinsky, Dmitri and Ludmilla	Pages from the life of Dmitri Shostakovich. London, 1980. Robert Hale
Volkov, Solomon	Testimony. The memoirs of Dmitri Shostakovich. London, 1979. Hamish Hamilton

The Music

Kay, Norman	Shostakovich. London, 1971. OUP
Macdonald, Malcolm	Dmitri Shostakovich. A complete catalogue. London, 1977. Boosey & Hawkes
Ottaway, Hugh	Shostakovich Symphonies. London, 1978. BBC

Russian History and Politics

Deutscher, Isaac	The Unfinished Revolution. London, 1975. OUP
Goldston, Robert	The Russian Revolution. London, 1967. J. M. Dent
Reed, John	Ten days that shook the world. London, 1978. Penguin
Salisbury, Harrison	The Siege of Leningrad. London, 1969. Secker & Warburg
Trotsky, Leon	My Life. London, 1971. Penguin
Westwood, J. N.	Russia 1917–1964. London, 1966. B. T. Batsford

Russian Art and Theatre

Eisenstein, Sergei — The Film Sense. London, 1963. Faber & Faber

Hoover, Marjorie L. — Meyerhold: The Art of Conscious Theatre. Amherst, U.S.A., 1974. University of Massachusetts Press

Milner, J. — Russian Revolutionary Art. London, 1979. Oresko Books

Russian Literature

Hingley, Ronald — Russian Writers and Soviet Society. London, 1979. Weidenfeld & Nicolson

Struve, Gleb — Russian Literature under Lenin and Stalin, 1917–1953. Oklahoma, U.S.A., 1971. University of Oklahoma Press

A Select Discography

The fifteen symphonies and string quartets, together with the six concertos (two each for piano, cello and violin) are recommended as the foundation of any representative collection of Shostakovich's music on record. A complete box set of the symphonies in which leading Soviet Russian orchestras are under the direction of five conductors, all of whom have been involved in Shostakovich premières at one time or another (Kondrashin, Svetlanov, Maxim Shostakovich, Mravinsky and Barshai) is currently available[1]. A number of alternative non Soviet recordings present themselves, with the widest choice in the fifth (no less than six recordings) and first and tenth symphonies (four in each case). The international, a-political appeal of the music is evident in its championship by conductors all over the world. For instance, Previn is a brilliant and passionate advocate of Nos. 4, 5, 6 and 8 in which he directs the Chicago Symphony Orchestra (in 4[2] and 5[3]) and the London Symphony Orchestra (in 5[4], 6[5] and 8[6]). The Finnish conductor, Paavo Berglund, already well known for his commitment to Sibelius, has recorded 5, 7 and 10 with the Bournemouth Symphony Orchestra: he and his orchestra should be heard before contemplating bigger names in the above works. A fine recording of No. 7 (coupled with the 'little' 9th) comes from Neumann and the Czech Philharmonic[7]. The doyen of our European symphonic conductors, Bernard Haitink, has embarked with the London Philharmonic Orchestra on a complete recording of the symphonies — so far we have Nos. 4[8], 10[9] and 15[10].

The string quartets Nos. 1–13 have been recorded complete by the (Soviet) Borodin String Quartet[11]. The Beethoven Quartet, for whom Shostakovich wrote nearly all his string quartets, has only recorded Nos. 14 and 15[12], which seems a regrettable state of affairs. In strong competition to the Russians is the complete set of 15 by the English Fitzwilliam Quartet[13], who bring a finely disciplined and committed intensity of feeling to this 'private' music. No doubt the composer, who very much admired the Fitzwilliam's playing of his late quartets, would have been delighted with their achievement had he lived to hear it.

There would appear to be no contestants ready to dispute the supremacy of Oistrakh and Rostropovich in the arena of the concertos for violin[14] and cello[15 and 16]. (The subtle second cello concerto is, it seems to me, unjustifiably overshadowed by the more popular No. 1.) The delightful second piano concerto has, on the other hand, attracted several protagonists, Bernstein amongst them[17]. On a record 'Shostakovich plays Shostakovich' (recorded in Paris in 1958)[18] the composer is the rather hectic, poker-faced soloist in this work and the first concerto (featuring also the trumpet as co-soloist with the string orchestra) which he wrote for himself in 1933.

Rozhdestvensky's revival of *The Nose* in 1974 was shortly afterwards recorded in close collaboration with the composer: it is an essential item, recorded with all the stereophonic liveliness of a stage performance[19]. The 1963 'blazing' revival of *Lady Macbeth* under its new title of *Katerina Ismailovna* was brought into the recording studio with the same stage cast under the direction of G. Provotorov[20]. These landmarks in the composer's early career show what a born opera composer was lost to Soviet Russia when Stalin sought to discipline the Shostakovich of 'Lady Macbeth' in 1936. Incidentally, the original 1936 version of the opera had now been recorded under the direction of Rostropovich in American exile, with his wife, Galina Vishnevskaya, in the title role[21]. Record enthusiasts are thus in a position to compare the two versions and draw their own conclusions.

It is only the formidable language barrier which delays a fuller appreciation, here and elsewhere, of the importance of Shostakovich the song composer. A recording of two late song cycles, the finely ironic 'Five Romances on texts from Krokodil' and the 'Four Verses of Capitan Lebjadkin' has been made by the singer Yevgeni Nesterenko who gave the Leningrad and Moscow premières of these pieces and worked with the composer on their interpretation. There is also to be enjoyed on this record the very unpompous 'Preface to the Complete Collection of my Works and brief Reflection apropos this Preface', Op.123 — a work belied by its ponderous title[22]. The same splendid Russian bass is to be heard in extended soliloquy in the monumental *Suite on Verses of Michelangelo*[23]. Here the composer seems to be bringing his life's work to a close as he broods darkly over the themes of Death and Immortality.

Finally, there is the sonata for viola and piano[24] recorded after the composer's death by its dedicatee, Fyodor Druzhinin with Michael Muntyan at the piano. This, Shostakovich's last completed composition, forms the peaceful coda to a turbulent creative life. Significantly enough, the last movement alludes to Beethoven's 'Moonlight' Sonata — a final act of homage to a great revolutionary artist from another age who was never far from the Soviet composer's thoughts.

Recordings referred to above

[1] SLS 5025 (26s. nas)
[2] ASD 3440
[3] ASD 3443
[4] GL 42690
[5] ASD 3029
[6] ASD 2917
[7] 110 1771-2 (4s. nas)
[8] SXL 6927
[9] SXL 6838
[10] SXL 6906
[11] SLS 879 (12s. nas)
[12] HQS 1362
[13] DSL 09; DSL 011; DSL 023; DSL 028 – 031
[14] ASD 2936
[15] 72081
[16] 2530 653
[17] 72170 or 73400
[18] SH 293
[19] SLS 5088 (4s. nas)
[20] SLS 5050 (8s)
[21] SLS 5157 (6s. nas)
[22] ASD 3700
[23] SLS 5078
[24] HQS 1369

A Note on Sources

This short Life and Times of Shostakovich is based on a compilation of material from many sources, some not readily available in this country. I have been guided by one leading principle: that, as far as possible, I should use as the substance of my story the original testimony of those who lived through those times and actually knew or met the composer. Thus I have drawn on poetry as well as newspaper reports, camera, cinema and poster images as well as the sayings of fellow artists, journalists, politicians and critics. Because a close family secrecy is understandably still preserved over so much of the composer's private life and thoughts I have frequently had to rely solely on the clues his music affords rather than the customary evidence of letters and diaries. (But here we are fortunate, because Shostakovich did use music as a means of private communication — almost as a code to be interpreted or deciphered.) On the other hand there is, of course, no lack of official verbal pronouncement from the composer himself which has been no less relevant to my story.

Shostakovich is the only great composer in the history of music whose creative development was demonstrably moulded by socio-political events and cultural ideologies pertaining to them. It is impossible to dicuss Shostakovich except in terms of the impact of these events on his career. Accordingly some attempt to summarise these events (conscious though I am of my deficiencies as a professional historian) has been made for the benefit of the general reader from the standpoint of Shostakovich's own musical documentary approach, which was — I take comfort from the fact — not necessarily a very sophisticated one. Thus my account of the two revolutions was based on the sequence of Shostakovich's own historical titles to the different movements in the programme symphonies Nos. eleven and twelve. To fill out this account, as well as using photographs I have drawn on the eye-witness accounts of Trotsky, John Reed and Lenin's widow while relying for the main outlines on such pre-eminently readable popular histories as those of Godston, H. G. Wells, Westwood and Floyd. The astute socio-analytical commentaries of Hingley, Struve, Werth and Deutscher were constantly at my elbow. In the field of Soviet Marxist-Leninist music analysis and criticism I have been able to study the writings of Sollertinsky and Asafiev — still largely unknown in the West, thanks to the help of my translator, Miss Jane Kentish.

This book could not have been written without frequent reference to Boris Schwarz's monumental History of Music and Musical Life in Soviet Russia, and the standard biographies (at present all out of print) by Seroff, Rabinovich and Martynov. Another valuable source of information on the composer'a life at the time of the first symphony is provided by the conductor Nicolai Malko in his book "A Certain Art" (also out of print). I am particularly grateful to the conductor's son, George Malko, for permission to quote material from his father's book as well as for the loan of the photograph.

The publication of the controversial Shostakovich-Volkov Memoirs in 1979 was an event that no serious student of Shostakovich could ignore. These memoirs have been disputed in the Soviet Union and questioned by certain leading authorities in the West. However, it seemed to me relevant to quote, where appropriate to my story, from a personal source which was indisputably close to the composer in his late years and who so obviously knew and understood something of the Soviet scene from a dissident Russo-Semitic angle. (It should be noted that Boris Schwarz, in his article on Shostakovich in the new Grove, is not prepared to dismiss Volkov's book as a fake, though one must remain uneasy about certain aspects of this fascinating publication.)

For the illustrations I owe a big debt of gratitude to the unfailing kindness and courtesy of Novosti Press Agency and the Society for Cultural Relations with the USSR, who have readily placed so much material at my disposal. I can only hope that I have used this material in a way which steers a reasonable course between sympathetic identification with the creative outlook of my subject (inseparable, as I have said, from Soviet ideology) and crude dogma, whether of one political persuasion or another.

Eric Roseberry
Croscombe, 1981

Acknowledgements and References

Acknowledgements are due for quotations from the following sources: G Abraham in BBC Radio 3 Talk 2 Nov 1979; *Anglo Soviet Journal Music Bulletin* London October 1954 by permission of The Society for Cultural Relations with the USSR; O Berggolts trans. D Weissbort *Post War Russian Poetry* London 1974; C Creighton *Musical Moments on Soviet TV* SCR Review May 1980; I Engelmann *Interview with Shostakovich* The Listener 14 Nov 1974; and *Music from the Flames* BBC film 1974; D Floyd from *Russia in Revolt* London 1969 by permission of Macdonald General Books; Alan George *Dmitry Shostakovich—A Personal Recollection* Cheltenham International Festival Programme Book 1976, by permission of the author; M Glenny in *Novy Mir 1925—1967* London 1972; J Goethe trans. P Wayne *Faust* London 1949; N Gogol trans. C J Hogarth *The Nose* London 1963; M Gorki *Literature and Life, A Selection from the Writings of M Gorki* Hutchinson International Authors 1946; T Grum-Grzhimailo trans. S Rosenberg *Leningrad's Sad Genius* Observer Colour Supplement 5 Dec 1971; R Hingley in *Russian Writers and Society 1917-1978* London 1979 by permission Weidenfeld and Nicolson; O Ivinskaya *A Captive of Time* London 1979 by permission of Collins Publishers; H Keller quoting in *Tempo 94* Autumn 1970; N Krupskaya *Memories of Lenin* London 1942 by permission of Lawrence and Wishart Ltd; Küchelbecker trans. V Vlazinskaya, booklet to recording of *Symphony No 14* Melodiya; A Laurentiev in *Alexander Rodchenko* ed. D Elliott, Museum of Modern Art Oxford 1979; R Layton Sleeve note for *Symphony No 4* EMI Melodiya; R Lee *Dmitri Shostakovich* New York Times 20 Dec 1931; A Mahler trans. B Creighton ed. D Mitchell *Gustav Mahler, Memories and Letters* London 1973 by permission of John Murray (Publishers) Ltd; N Malko *A Certain Art* New York 1966 © George Malko by permission; I Martynov *Dmitry Shostakovitch, The man and his Work* New York 1974; D McLellan Marx Glasgow 1945; D Mitchell in *Tempo* No 120 March 1977 and *Shostakovitch and his Symphonies* in *Aldeburge Anthology* ed R Blythe London 1972, both by permission of the author; R Moisenko in *Realist Music* London 1949; V Nabokov *Nikolay Gogol* London 1973 by permission of Weidenfeld and Nicolson; G Norris *The Nose* Musical Times May 1979; H Ottaway, sleeve note to *The Fools Song* Melodiya, and *Shostakovich Symphonies* London 1978; B Pasternak trans. A Brown *Safe Conduct* London 1959 by permission of Granada Publishing Ltd and *Dr Zhivago* Collins 1958; P Pears *Moscow Christmas 1966* Private publication by permission of Sir Peter Pears; Preface to MCA edition of Symphony No 10; S Prokofiev *Autobiography* Moscow; A Pushkin trans. J Fennell *The Bronze Horseman* London 1964; D Rabinovich *Dmitry Shostakovitch* London 1959 by permission of Lawrence and Wishart Ltd; J Reed *Ten Days that shook the World* London 1978; H Salisbury *Visit with Dmitri Shostakovich* New York Times 8 Aug 1954 by permission of the author; E H Schloss *Philadelphia Inquirer* quoted on sleeve note of CBS recording of first cello concerto; B Schwarz in *Music and Musical Life in Soviet Russia 1917–1970* London 1972 by permission of Hutchinson Publishing Group Ltd; V Seroff in *Dmitri Shostakovitch, The Life and Background of a Soviet Composer* New York 1947 reprinted by Books for Libraries Press, distributed by Arno Press Inc. D Shostakovich in *Russian Symphony* Philosophical Library New York 1947 and in *Sovetskaya Muzika* 1946; M Slonin in *Soviet Russian Literature* New York 1977; I Sollertinsky trans. J Kentish *Mahler* Leningrad 1932 and *Symphonic Types of Dramaturgy* (both unpublished in English); A Solzhenitsyn *One Word of Truth* London 1972; I Stravinsky and R Craft *Expositions and Developments* London 1962 and *Dialogues and a Diary* London 1968 by permission of Faber and Faber Ltd; G Struve in *Russian Literature under Lenin and Stalin* Oklahoma 1971; L Trotsky *My Life: An Attempt at an Autobiography* © Pathfinder Press Inc 1970 reprinted by permission of Penguin Books Ltd; S Volkov *Testimony: The Memoirs of Shostakovich* London 1979 reprinted by permission of Hamish Hamilton Ltd; and *Shostakovich and 'Tea for Two'* Musical Quarterly April 1978; A Werth *Leningrad* London 1944 and Moscow '41 London, 1942 by permission of Hamish Hamilton Ltd and *Musical Uproar in Moscow* London 1949 by permission of Turnstile Press Ltd; H G Wells *A Short History of the World* London 1965 by permission of A P Watt Ltd; J Westwood *Russia 1917–1964* London 1966; G Widdicombe *Three Friends* Observer 22 Nov 1977, by permission of The Observer; Yevtushenko trans. M Haywood *Post War Russian Poetry* London 1974.

Index

Illustrations are indicated by bold type

Abraham, Gerald 94, 138
Akhmatova, Ann 28, 59, 87, 108, 114
Alexandrov, Georgi **129**
Annensky, Innokenti 30
Apollinaire, Guillaume 169
Asafiev, Boris 63, 70, 84, 93, 124
Aurora (Battleship) **51**, 53

Bach, Johann Sebastian 56, 63, 128, 130
Balakirev, Mili 32
Bartok, Bela 62, 98
Beethoven, Ludwig van 11, 15, 38, 41, 53, 56, 62, 63, **63**, 75, 88, **89**, 90, 111, 112, 113, 128, 137, 166
Beethoven Quartet 100, 111, 127, **128**, 132, 166, 169, 174
Benois, Alexander 26
Berg, Alban 84, 98, 144, 179
Beria, Lavrenti 132
Blok, Alexander 30, 70
Bloody Sunday 16, 20, 22
Bogdanov-Berezovsky, Valerian 102, 105
Borissovsky, Vadim 170
Borodin, Alexander 38, 40
Brahms, Johannes 56
Brecht, Berthold 87
Brezhnev, Leonid 165
Britten, Benjamin 62, 85, **159**, 160, 161, 165, 168, 169
Bruckner, Anton 11, 93
Busoni, Ferruccio 56
Byron, George, Lord 70

Chamberlain, Neville 97
Chaplin, Charlie 9
Chopin, Frederic 56
Copland, Aaron **150**
Count de Witte 23

Debussy, Claude 26, 27, 87
Diaghilev, Sergei 26
Dickens, Charles 8, 15
Dostoyevsky, Fedor 8, 30, 173
Druzhinin, F. 176
Dzerzhinsky, Ivan 138

Eisenstein, Sergei 11, 18, 22, 77, 124
Engelmann, Ian 46, 173

Fadeyev, Alexander 92, 135
Father Gapon **17**, 18
Fitzwilliam Quartet, The 168, 170, **170**
Foss, Lucas **150**
Franco, General 97

Galileo 13, 154
Glazunov, Alexander 26, 58, 60, **61**, 62, 70
Glazunov Quartet, The 94
Gliasser, Ignatiy Albertovich 54, **54**, 56
Glinka, Mikhail 33, 173
Gogol, Nikolai 9, 70, 82, 83, 109, 110, 131, 174
Gorki, Maxim 90
Goya, Francisco 15

Handel, George F. 56
Hegel, Georg 11, 92, 94
Henderson, Robert 152
Hindemith, Paul 62, 70, 87, 98, 130
Hingley, Ronald 110, 127, 131
Hitler, Adolph 11, 87, 96, 97, 98, 100, 111, 152

Igumnov, Konstantin 127
Ivinskaya, Olga 127, 135

Kabalevsky, Dmitri 121
Karajan, Herbert von **142**
Keldysh, Yuri 130
Kerensky, A. 49, 51, 52
Khachaturian, Aram 116, 121, 138, 140
Khrennikov, Tikhon **121**, 122, 140, 149, **157**
Khrushchev, Nikita 12, 132, 145, 146, 149, **151**, 152, 165
Kirov, Sergei **64**, 11, 145
Kokaoulin, Jasha (uncle) 33, 72
Kokaoulin, Nadejda (aunt) 24, 33, 39, 60, 72
Kokaoulin, Tanya (cousin) 72
Kokaoulin, Vassily (maternal grandfather) 33
Kondrashin, Kyril 152, 154
Kornilov, General 49
Kosygin, Alexei 165
Kremlev, Yuli 143
Krupskaya, N. (Lenin's widow) 20, 47
Kubatsky, Viktor 85
Kussevitsky, Sergei 41
Kustodiev, B. M. 55, 56, 57, 58, 67

Lenin, Vladimir 10, 20, 41, 46, **47**, **48**, 49, 52, **52**, 54, 59, 62, 65, **65**, 67, 69, 82, 87, 99, 101, 115, 132, 138, 145, 146, 152
Liszt, Franz 15, 63, 137
Lunacharsky, Anatole 10, 63, 69, 81

Mahler, Gustav 11, 15, 26, 30, 63, 70, 74, 84, 87, 90, 93, 95, 99, 107, 175
Malenkov, Georgi 132
Malevich, Kazimir 10
Malko, Nikolai 32, 71, **71**, 72, 74, 75, 80, 82
Mandelstam, Osip 135
Marx, Karl 11, 58, 67, 92, 93
Mayakovsky, Vladimir 10, 67, 77, 78, **78**, 80, 99
Mendeleyev, Dmitri 37
Meyerhold, Vsevolod 11, 28, 40, 75, 77, **80**, 87, 93, 98, 109
Miaskovsky, Nikolai 124, **124**
Mitropoulos, Dimitri 144
Molotov, Vyacheslav 132
Mozart, Wolfgang Amadeus 38, 154
Mravinsky, Yevgeny **91**, 92, **117**, 132
Muradeli, Vano 117, 118, **119**, 120, 121
Mussolini, Benito 96, 97
Mussorgsky, Modest 40, 168

Nabokov, Vladimir 30
Napoleon 100, 108
Nesterenko, Yevgeni 161
Newman, Ernest 107
Nikolayev, Leonid 61, **61**, 62, 67, 70
Nikolayeva, Tatiana 128
Oistrakh, David **117**, 124, 143, 144, 149

Pasternak, Boris 9, 15, 18, 19, 28, 46, 65, 127, 135, 137, 149
Pasteur, Louis 13
Pears, Sir Peter 161
Peter the Great 14, 28, 31, 41, 95
Picasso, Pablo 96, 97
Popov, Gavril 121
The Potemkin (Battleship) **21**, 22, **22**, **77**
Prokofiev, Sergei 12, 14, 26, **26**, 44, 61, 70, 90, 116, 120, 121, 122, 124
Pushkin, Alexander 30, 39

Rabinovich, D. 38, 99, 100, 102, 112, 127, 145
Rachlin, Nikolai **148**
Rachmaninov, Sergei 145
Rasputin, Grigori 41, 42
Rastrelli, Bartolommeo 31, 32, 95
Ravel, Maurice 26
Reger, Max 26
Repin, Ilya 169
Richter, Sviatoslav 124
Rimsky Korsakov, Nikolai 26, **26**, 39, 40, 58, 60, 140
Rodchenko, Alexander 10, 28, 57, 76, 77
Rossini, Gioacchino 157, 173
Rostropovich, Mstislav 124, 151, 161, **162**, 163, 167, 168, 171, 176
Rozhdestvensky, Gennadi 175, **177**

Salisbury, Harrison 140, 141
Schoenberg, Arnold 26, 87, 98, 163, 165, 166
Schumann, Robert 56, 125
Schwarz, Boris 63, 133, 144, 154, 158
Scriabin, Alexander 27, **40**, 41, 61, 70
Shakespeare, William 13, 70, 90
Shaporin, Yuri 121, 140
Shaw, Bernard 40
Shchedrin, Rodion 131
Shebalin, Vissarion 121
Shostakovich, Dmitri Boleslavovich (father) 34, **34**, 39, 58, 59
Shostakovich, Dmitri Dmitrievich passim **37**, **54**, **55**, **73**, **80**, **83**, **89**, **101**, **102**, **110**, **117**, **118**, **126**, **128**, **129**, **142**, **150**, **155**, **159**, **160**, **162**, **170**, **173**, **175**, **177**
- Aphorisms, Op.13 15, 82
- The Bedbug, Op.19 67, 77, 78
- Cello Concerto No.1, Op.107 14, 150
- Cello Concerto No.2, Op.126 14, 15, 161, 163
- Children's Notebook, Op.69 112
- The Dragonfly and the Ant (No. 1 of Two Fables of Krilov, Op.4) 72
- Eight Preludes, Op.2 57, 63
- Four verses of Captain Lebjadkin, Op.146 173
- From Jewish Folk Poetry, Op.79 126
- Funeral March in memory of the victims of the October Revolution 7, 45, **46**
- The Gamblers 109, 164
- The Golden Age, Op.22 80
- The Gypsies (after Pushkin) 39
- Katerina Ismailova, Op.29/114 12, 157, **164**
- Lady Macbeth of the Mtensk District, Op.29 9, 11, 12, 84, 85, 86, 87, 93, 118, 120, 155, 161, **164**
- Leningrad Symphony – see Symphony No.7
- The Nose, Op.15 9, 82, 83, 84, 86, 109, 164, 174, **176**, 177
- Piano Concerto No.2, Op.102 145
- Piano Quintet, Op.57 100
- Piano Sonata No.2, Op.61 62
- Piano Trio No. 2, Op. 67 111, 112, 132
- Preface to the complete collection of my works and brief reflections apropos this Preface, Op.123 149, 161
- Scherzo in F sharp minor, Op.1 72
- Soldier 7
- Sonata for cello and piano, Op.40 85
- Song of the Motherland, Op74 125
- String Quartet No.1, Op.49 38, 88, 94, 95, 98, 99, 111
- String Quartet No.2 Op. 68 111, 112
- String Quartet No.3, Op.73 127, 144
- String Quartet No.4, Op.83 125, 132
- String Quartet No.5, Op.92 125, 132, 138, 144
- String Quartet No.7, Op.108 14, 144
- String Quartet No.8, Op.110 13, 151
- String Quartet No.9, Op.117 14
- String Quartet No.11, Op.122 161, 169
- String Quartet No.12, Op.133 166, 169
- String Quartet No.13, Op.138 14, 168, 169, 170
- String Quartet No.14, Op.142 169, 176
- String Quartet No.15, Op.144 14, 88, 176, 178, 181
- String Quartet No.15, Op.144 14, 88, 174, 175, 178
- Suite on Verses of Michelangelo, Op.145/145a 15, 173, 174, 175
- Symphony No.1, Op.10 62, 63, 70–74, 75, 84

Symphony No.2, Op. 14 8, 43, 81, 82
Symphony No.3, Op.20 **164**
Symphony No.4, Op.43 11, 12, 87, 88–94, 98, 125, 137, 152, **153**
Symphony No.5, Op.47 11, 15, 38, 62, 87, 88–92, 94, 95, 98, 99
Symphony No.6, Op.54 15, 92, 95, 99–100
Symphony No.7, Op.60 11, 12, 15, 62, 95, 101–108, 109, 111, 112, 113
Symphony No.8, Op.65 11, 12, 15, 92, 95, 108, 109, 112, 113
Symphony No.9, Op.70 9, 12, 15, 92, 112–113
Symphony No.10, Op.93 12, 15, 92, 100, 125, 132–140, 142, 143, 144
Symphony No.11, Op.103 8, 13, 15, 19, **148**, 149
Symphony No.12, Op.112 13, 15, 43, 46, 47, 53, 149, 152
Symphony No.13, Op.113 13, 15, 152–159
Symphony No.14, Op.135 9, 14, 161, 168, 178
Symphony No.15, Op.141 9, 14, 59, 173, 175
Symphony No.16 175
Tahiti Trot, Op.16 (Tea for Two) 77, 80, 82
Theme with Variations, Op.3 63
Three Fantastic Dances, Op.5 63
Twenty-Four Preludes and Fugues, Op.34 138
Viola Sonata, Op.147 14, 62, 174, 175
Violin Concerto No.1, Op.77 125, 144, 149
Shostakovich family 33, 39, 59, 67, 161
Shostakovich, Galya (daughter) 98, 11, 112, **118**, 144, 145
Shostakovich, Irena (third wife) 14, 145, 160, **174**, 174, 176
Shostakovich, Margarita (second wife) 145
Shostakovich,Marusia (sister) 15, 37, **37**, 59, 67
Shostakovich, Maxim (son) 98, 108, 111, **118**, 144, 145, 168, 173, **175**
Shostakovich, Nina (first wife) 14, 75, **83**, 98, 108, 144
Shostakovich, Sophia (mother) 33, 34, 37, **37**, 59, 67, 68, 71, 110, 144
Shostakovich, Zoya (sister) 37, **37**, 59, 67
Sibelius, Jean 98
Siege of Leningrad 12, **106**, **107**
Sollertinsky, Ivan 11, **83**, 84, 87, 90, 93, 99, 111, 124
Solzhenitsyn, Alexander 9, 113, 152, 168
Stalin, Joseph 9, 10, 11, 12, 14, **64**, 65, **65**, 75, 84, 85, 86, 87, 88, 90, 95, 97, 98, 99, 110, 111, 112, 113, 114, 116, 117, 118, 120, 122, 123, 125, 127, 131, 132, 133, 134, 135, 137, 138, **139**, 145, 146, 152
Stalin Prize 100, 141
Steinberg, Maximilian 26, 58, 61, 70, 140
Stiedry, Fritz 87
Stokowski, Leopold 75
Stolypin, Peter 26
Strauss, Richard 26, 87
Stravinsky, Igor **26**, 26, 30, 31, 70, 87, **157**, 159

Tchaikovsky, Peter 11, 34, 38, 40, 70, 90, 93
Tolstoy, Lev 13, 15, 33, 93, 154
Toscanini, Arturo 107
Trotsky, Leon 16, 24, 25, 26, 49, 52, 59, 65, 87, 97, 138
Tsar Alexander II 36
Tsar Alexander III 32
Tsar Nicholas I 33, 82
Tsar Nicholas II 16, 18, 19, 20, 22, 23, 24, 25, 26, 33, 41, 43, 46, 51, 56, 59
Tsarina Alexandra 41, 42
Tukhachevsky, M. Marshall 146

Vaughan Williams, Ralph 98
Vishnevskaya, Galina **164**, 181
Volkov, Solomon 8, 12, 43, 56, 62, 67, 92, 99, 108, 109, 112, 135, 145, 159, 175, 181

Wagner, Richard 174
Walter, Bruno 74
Walton, William 98
Weill, Kurt 87
Werth, Alexander 30, 41, 109, 116, 127
Wilde, Oscar 40

Yarustovsky, Boris 140
Yesenin, Sergei 143, 146
Yevtushenko, Yevgeni 13, **146**, 154, 155

Zamyatin, Yevgeni 67
Zdhanov, Andrei 12, 85, 114, 115, **115**, 116, 117, 118, 120, 121, 122, 125, 128, 132, 133, 138, 140, 146, 166
Zoshchenko, Mikhail 114